Computer Art and Illusions

Programs for Artisans and Craftspeople

Timothy Masters

Great effort has been undertaken in ensuring that the content of this book, including all associated computer code, is as close to correct as possible. However, errors and omissions are inevitable in a work of this extent; they are surely present. Neither this book nor the associated computer code are meant as professional advice. No guarantee is made that this material is free of errors and omissions, and the reader assumes full liability for any losses associated with use of this material. The algorithms described in this book and implemented in theassociated programs are experimental and not vetted by any outside experts or tested in the crucible of time. Please treat them accordingly.

About the author:

Timothy Masters received a PhD in mathematical statistics with a specialization in numerical computing. Since then he has continuously worked as an independent consultant for government and industry. His early research involved automated feature detection in high-altitude photographs while he developed applications for flood and drought prediction, detection of hidden missile silos, and identification of threatening military vehicles. Later he worked with medical researchers in the development of computer algorithms for distinguishing between benign and malignant cells in needle biopsies. For the last twenty years he has focused primarily on methods for evaluating automated financial market trading systems. He has authored numerous books on practical applications of predictive modeling as well as automated trading of financial markets.

Readers of this computer art book may be especially interested in his *Modern Stereogram Algorithms for Art and Scientific Visualization*, available from all major online booksellers. More details concerning all of his nonfiction and fiction books can be found on his personal website.

The software referenced in this text may be downloaded from the author's website:
TimothyMasters.info

Contents

1

Introduction

I love artistic craft projects, especially in wood. However, I am completely devoid of ability to draw or paint; if I were to draw a tree it would be two curved lines for the trunk and a blob on top. The people that emerge from my drawing efforts are stick figures. Yet I often want to decorate my wood and 3D printed creations with pretty artwork. It occurred to me some time ago that I might be able to put my mathematical and programming abilities to work in ways that use the computer to do the drawing for me. After writing a few interesting programs to do just that I decided to make the executables and complete source code available to the public as free downloads from my website, and document their inner workings in an inexpensive book. So here it is. This book and program set includes:

Vortex - This program creates an image of a vortex plunging into an abyss. A black-and-white checkerboard is distorted in such a way as to give the appearance of a hole into which objects can be sucked. If this pattern is transferred to a large floor covering, examples of which can be seen for sale on the internet, the effect can be striking.

Blocks - All you need is a quantity of three slightly differently shaped and colored parallelograms, easily mass produced, to create an impressive 3D illusion. I have seen woodworkers making and selling beautiful cutting boards in this pattern. A little careful veneer work can produce gorgeous covers for wood boxes. This program provides the exact shapes needed, and lets the artist visualize what the end product would look like. The size and shape of the illusory cubes, as well as the viewing angle, can be adjusted by the artist for maximum creative control.

Julia - Programs for visualizing Mandelbrot and Julia sets were a dime a dozen in the 90's, and are still somewhat available on the internet. My program goes beyond the common versions in two ways. First, it uses a very advanced algorithm that can produce only binary (such as black and white) images of these sets, but it does so with extreme detail, reaching resolutions far beyond what can be obtained with the usual 'dwell escape' algorithm. Second, it generalizes Mandelbrot and Julia sets to the quaternion (four dimensional) domain, lets the user define a 3D cross sectional object from the 4D set, and then it uses ray tracing to display this cross section with white or colored lights arrayed in any of several user-defined positions. Julia sets in four dimensions have a strange, almost creepy otherworldly appearance and can make for highly unusual decorative patterns.

Lin - Aristid Lindenmayer devised a mathematical language that can be used to describe the growth and structure of plants. Just a few lines of Lindenmayer code can serve to rigorously describe trees, bushes, flowers, and even alien-looking plant-like creations. The *Lin* program supports three levels of Lindenmayer systems:

> 1) Simple edge replacement algorithms produce snowflake curves, Koch curves, dragon curves, Sierpinski gaskets, and so forth. This primitive but often lovely family of curves makes fabulous decorative ornamentation.

> 2) Two-dimensional axial generation produces flat but interesting plant-like objects, with strikingly realistic branching patterns. These simple plant representations make perfect focal points for handcrafted items.

> 3) Three-dimensional axial generation can produce shockingly realistic plants and flowers, reminiscent of plant sketches made by professional artists and illustrators. The *Lin* program allows for an almost unlimited number of productions, up to ten different colors for different plant parts, and even up to three different versions of each production, with versions randomly selected according to user-specified probabilities. This lets the artist create entire fields of plants, all of the same 'species', but no two exactly alike.

All of these programs run under 64-bit Windows. The source code compiles with Microsoft Visual C++ 2019 and probably most other modern C++ compilers (although I have not tested the code on any other compilers). The executables as well as complete source code can be downloaded for free from my website, TimothyMasters.info. This book provides detailed explanations of the algorithms as well as tutorial examples. Enjoy.

2

The Vortex Illusion

The first time I saw one of those rugs that give the illusion that there is a huge sucking hole in the middle of the floor, my jaw dropped. Once I got over my awe of how real the effect appeared, I resolved that I would figure out how such an amazing image was created. The math is not terribly difficult, but it is a bit tedious and has a few gotchas to consider. I'll now go through the math one step at a time, including C++ source code to implement the illusion. A complete program that allows user-specified view positions and display options concludes the presentation. This program and complete source code can be downloaded from my website.

The Vortex Shape

I wrote the program in such a way that the user can easily swap in his or her own vortex shape code. However, I believe that my version is more than adequate. Please look at Figure 2.2 below.

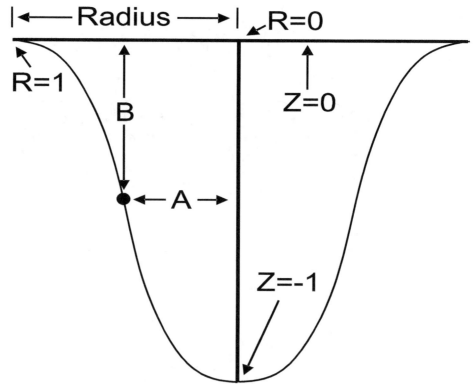

Figure 2.2: The vortex profile, seen from any point on the Z=0 plane

That figure is a side view of the boundary of the circularly symmetric vortex as seen from any point on the XY plane (i.e. the plane for which $Z=0$). The boundary of the vortex is defined as the function $Z=f(radius)$. In order for the vortex shape to be pleasing to the eye and compatible with the rest of the program it must satisfy certain reasonable properties:

- Assume $0 <= R$ (the radius) $<= 1$
  The radius ranges from 0 at the center of the vortex to 1 at its rim.

- $-1 <= Z(R) <= 0$ for all R
  No part of the vortex lies above the XY plane or below -1.

- $Z(1) = 0$
  The top rim of the vortex lies on the XY plane.

- $Z'(1) = 0$
  The first derivative of $Z(R)$ at the top rim is zero (the edge is flat).

- $Z(0) = -1$
  The vortex reaches its lowest point at the center.

- $Z(R)$ is a monotonically increasing function of R.

My first attempt at a profile curve was the simple function shown in Equation (2.1). This equation satisfies all of the properties above and produces a satisfactory vortex. However, it takes too long to drop off around the rim, resulting in a vortex that is smaller in diameter than is visually appealing.

$$Z(R) = -(1-R)^3 \qquad (2.1)$$

I found that the appearance is helped by breaking the profile into two parts, an upper part that plunges quickly, and a lower part that completes the function in a way that satisfies all of the required properties. This transition point is shown as a small black circle in Figure 2.2, happening at a radius of A with a corresponding $Z=-B$. Designate the upper part as $Z_1(R)$ and the lower part as $Z_2(R)$.

This separation requires several more properties that involve the individual functions and whose meanings should be clear as long as the prior properties are understood:

- $Z_1(A) = Z_2(A) = -B$

- $Z_1(1) = 0$

- $Z'_1(1) = 0$

- $Z_2(0) = -1$

Note that I do not require equality of the first derivatives at the transition point. Fine graphics work would demand this in order to avoid the appearance of a sharp corner. However, for this application the derivatives are very close for reasonable values of A and B. In fact, I set $A=B=0.5$, in which case the derivatives are equal at the junction! Modifying Equation (2.1) to produce two separate equations that satisfy the extra properties is straightforward, so I won't present it here. The final equations are shown below.

$$Z_1(R) = -B\left(1 - \left[\frac{R-A}{1-A}\right]\right)^3 \qquad (2.2)$$

$$Z_2(R) = (1-B)\left(\frac{R}{A}\right)^3 - 1 \qquad (2.3)$$

Code For Computing The Vortex Boundary

The C++ code for computing the Z coordinate of the vortex boundary, given the radius in the range 0 (the center) to 1 (the boundary), is shown below. First we check to see if the caller has specified a radius beyond 1, in which case we return 0, the *XY* plane. Otherwise we decide which part of the curve we are in, and evaluate the appropriate equation. This is such simple code that translation to another language should be trivial.

```
#define CURVE_A 0.5
#define CURVE_B 0.5

double curve ( double radius )
{
  double x ;

  if (radius > 1.0)
    return 0.0 ;

  if (radius >= CURVE_A) {   // Upper curve, Z1
    x = 1.0 - (radius - CURVE_A) / (1.0 - CURVE_A) ;
    return -CURVE_B * x * x * x ;
    }

  else {          // Lower curve, Z2
    x = radius / CURVE_A ;
    return (1.0 - CURVE_B) * x * x * x - 1.0 ;
    }
}
```

The Projection Algorithm

This section discusses how to determine the set of exact locations (X, Y, Z) on the vortex boundary that the eye sees. To understand the basis of this algorithm, see Figure 2.3, which is a view from the $+X$ axis looking directly toward the origin $(0, 0, 0)$.

Because the vortex is circularly symmetric, without loss of generality we can assume that the X coordinate of the eye is zero. The eye Y is assumed to be negative or zero, and to avoid numerical difficulties we assume the eye Z is greater than one. The viewing window is the plane through the origin that is perpendicular to the ray from the eye to the origin. The elevation angle of the eye above the XY plane is theta (θ).

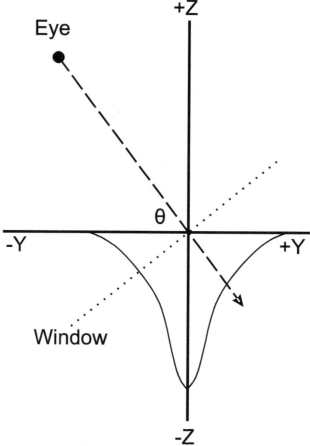

Figure 2.3: The vortex, eye, and viewing window

The eye 'sees' the vortex through a hypothetical viewing window. Each (*Row, Col*) location in this window corresponds to the vortex boundary location at which the ray from the eye, through (*Row, Col*), intersects the vortex boundary. In order to generate an image of the vortex, the window is partitioned into a fine-resolution grid, with *Row* and *Col* ranging from approximately –1 to 1. The center of the window is at (0, 0), positive rows are in the 'up' direction, and positive columns are in the 'right' direction, relative to an eye for which up is +Z / +Y and right is +X.

Note that most of the time the ray from the eye through (*Row, Col*) will intersect the vortex boundary exactly once, moving from 'above' the vortex to 'below'. However, especially if the eye is low (theta is small) the ray can intersect the vortex boundary three times, passing from the 'above' side to the 'below' side, then quickly passing to 'above' again, before traversing the wide inner expanse of the vortex and finally exiting permanently to the 'below' side. It's vital to understand (and a major nuisance!) that in case of multiple intersections, we are interested in only the one closest to the eye, because that is the one that the eye 'sees'. The other intersections are hidden from the eye.

Let the vector **EYE**=(EYE_X, EYE_Y, EYE_Z) be the (X, Y, Z) coordinates of the eye, recalling that for this application the eye's X will always be assumed to be zero. Let **W**=(W_X, W_Y, W_Z) be the (X, Y, Z) coordinates of a (*Row, Col*) point on the window. Let delta (Δ) be the vector that runs from the eye to the (*Row, Col*) point on the window, as shown in Equation (2.4). Then we can define any point **P** along this line or its extension in terms of a parameter *t*. This is shown in Equation (2.5). Note that when *t*=0 we are at the eye, and when *t*=1 we are on the window.

$$\Delta = W - EYE \tag{2.4}$$

$$P = EYE + t\Delta \tag{2.5}$$

Before we can use this approach to locate points along the eye-to-window ray we must know how to compute **W** from **EYE** and (*Row, Col*). An examination of Figure 2.3 shows that this is just basic trigonometry, as expressed in the following four equations.

$$\theta = \arctan\left(\frac{EYE_Z}{-EYE_Y}\right) \tag{2.6}$$

$$W_X = Col \tag{2.7}$$

$$W_Y = Row\,\sin(\theta) \tag{2.8}$$

$$W_z = Row\,\cos(\theta) \tag{2.9}$$

Assume that the user has specified **EYE**, and we want to examine the view window pixel at (*Row, Col*). Suppose we specify some value for the parameter *t*. The preceding equations can be used to compute the **P** that corresponds to this *t*. The *X* and *Y* coordinates of this point along the viewing ray tell us how far we are from the center of the vortex, as shown in Equation (2.10), and that in turn can tell us the *Z* location on the boundary of the vortex that corresponds to this *X, Y* location. This latter equation may be the simple shape of Equation (2.1) on Page 11, or it may be the split shape of Equations (2.2) and (2.3), or it may be your own curve that satisfies the required properties.

$$R = \sqrt{P_X{}^2 + P_Y{}^2} \tag{2.10}$$

This gives us one *Z*, that for the vortex boundary. Equation (2.5) gives us the *Z* of the point on the view ray that corresponds to this *t*. *When the view ray intersects the vortex boundary, these two values will be equal.* Thus, we need to find the value of *t* that makes these values equal, and if there are multiple values (intersections) we must find the smallest such *t*.

With this in mind, we need to have a subroutine that is given **EYE**, (*Row, Col*), and *t*, and returns the difference between these two values of *Z*. This subroutine will be used by a root finder that holds the eye and pixel fixed and finds the smallest root *t*.

Code For Finding the Z Difference

The following routine uses Equations (2.4) through (2.10) to compute and return the difference between view ray's Z and the vortex boundary's Z. The last four calling parameters require special explanation. The three components of delta do not depend on t; they are defined strictly by the eye and the window pixel. They are relatively slow to compute, because they require the inverse tangent function. This subroutine will be called many times with the same eye and window pixel, just varying t. So rather than computing the same values over and over, we pass pointers to the delta components and save them in the calling routine. The flag first_call is set to *True* the first time this subroutine is called with a new eye and window pixel, and this causes delta to be computed. Subsequent calls have the flag set to *False*, avoiding expensive recomputation.

```
double find_diff (
    double y_eye ,        // <= 0
    double z_eye ,        // > 1
    double row ,          // Row location in view window
    double col ,          // And column; often between about -1 and 1
    double t ,            // Relative length of ray; 0 at eye and 1 at window
    int first_call ,      // Flag: First call with this eye and window pixel?
    double *x_delta ,     // Work areas saved by caller
    double *y_delta ,
    double *z_delta
    )
{
    double theta, x_window, y_window, z_window ;
    double x_terminus, y_terminus, z_terminus, radius ;

    if (first_call) { // Delta does not depend on t, so compute it only once
        theta = atan2 ( z_eye , -y_eye ) ;     // Equation (2.6)
        x_window = col ;                       // Equation (2.7)
        y_window = row * sin ( theta ) ;       // Equation (2.8)
        z_window = row * cos ( theta ) ;       // Equation (2.9)

        *x_delta = x_window ;                  // Equation (2.4)
        *y_delta = y_window - y_eye ;
        *z_delta = z_window - z_eye ;
        }
```

```
// If z_delta is not negative, we are looking at or above the horizon
// so the ray cannot possibly intersect the vortex.

if (*z_delta >= 0.0)    // Projection from eye to window pixel rising!
    return 1.e60 ;      // Flag that we will never intersect (above horizon)

x_terminus = t * *x_delta ;              // Equation (2.5)
y_terminus = t * *y_delta + y_eye ;
z_terminus = t * *z_delta + z_eye ;


radius = sqrt ( x_terminus * x_terminus + y_terminus * y_terminus ) ; // Equation (2.10)
return z_terminus - curve ( radius ) ;    // Difference between the two Z values, want 0
}
```

The code just shown is mostly a straightforward implementation of the prior equations. There is just one abnormal situation that we must be prepared for. The importance of this situation will become clear in the next section. Suppose the eye is very low (theta is small). The viewing window will be almost vertical. If the user specifies a maximum row that is large, it can happen that the ray projecting from the eye to a high row in the window will be parallel to the horizon or even rising, meaning that the ray will never intersect the vortex boundary. This will cause an infinite loop in the root finder as it searches in vain for an intersection. We must prevent that from happening by checking the sign of the Z component of delta. Normally it will be negative, meaning that as t increases the ray will move downward, eventually piercing the vortex boundary, or at least piercing the XY plane outside the vortex. If it is not negative there's no point in searching for an intersection that does not exist!

Note that I use the atan2() function rather than the simpler atan(). This is because it's legal for the user to specify y_eye=0. There's no simple way to handle this with atan(), but it's legal with atan2().

Finding the Smallest Root

If we could be assured that the projected ray intersects the vortex boundary at only one point (the Z-difference equation has just one root) we could find that unique root quickly with any of a number of excellent root-finding algorithms. Unfortunately, there can be as many as three roots, and it is imperative that we find only the smallest. I made a few attempts to devise a clever and fast way to find the smallest root, but the equation is not simple and the roots can have widely variable spacing. All I could come up with is a way to compute a reasonable lower bound on the smallest root. So I begin with that lower bound and advance *t* very slowly until it switches sign, and return the midpoint as the smallest root. It's clumsy but it appears to work correctly, and it's not so slow that it presents a practical problem. Here is the code, and an explanation follows.

```
double find_t (
   double y_eye ,   // <= 0
   double z_eye ,   // > 1
   double row ,     // Row location in view window
   double col       // And column
   )
{
   int i;
   double eye_length, increment, lower, upper, lower_f, upper_f ;
   double x_delta, y_delta, z_delta ;

   eye_length = sqrt ( y_eye * y_eye + z_eye * z_eye ) ;
   increment = 0.001 / eye_length ;

   lower = 1.0 - (-y_eye / z_eye) / eye_length ;      // Decent approximation
   lower *= 0.99 ;                                     // Safety factor

   lower_f = find_diff ( y_eye, z_eye, row, col, lower, 1, &x_delta, &y_delta, &z_delta ) ;

   if (lower_f > 1.e50) // Looking above horizon?
      return 1.e60 ;

   assert ( lower_f > 0.0 ) ;
```

```
/*
   Loop until we go from positive to negative.
   The loop limit is for insurance only and should never be hit.
*/

   for (i=0 ; i<10000000 ; i++) {    // I can't imagine ever hitting this limit
      upper = lower + increment ;
      upper_f = find_diff( y_eye, z_eye, row, col, upper, 0, &x_delta, &y_delta, &z_delta ) ;
      if (upper_f <= 0.0)
         break ;
      lower = upper ;
      lower_f = upper_f ;
      }

   assert (i < 10000000) ;

   return  0.5 * (lower + upper) ; // It's not worth tangent interpolation
}
```

The first step is to decide on the increment size and then come up with a lower bound on t that is as large as possible, thereby minimizing the number of steps required to find the smallest root. Naturally, zero would be a lower bound, because the eye is by definition above the XY plane. But we can do better.

Recall that t is the length of the projection relative to the length of the vector connecting the eye to the window. This length is equal to the length of the eye vector at the center of the window, and slightly greater for other locations on the window. So we should make the increment inversely related to the length of the eye vector, thus making the search resolution at least roughly independent of the eye location. This is done by first computing **eye_length** and then **increment**. The value 0.001 is a good compromise between speed and accuracy; feel free to adjust it if you wish, though I see no reason to do so.

The lower bound computed in the code came about from a combination of trigonometric intuition and heuristics. I tested it for a wide variety of eye positions and window pixels, and in most of my tests it proved to be excellent, just slightly smaller than the smallest root, although in some extreme situations it was excessively but unavoidably small.

We initialize the root finding by computing the Z difference at this lower bound. Recall that find_diff() returns 1.e60 if we are looking above the horizon, so we check for that and immediately return a flag indicating this situation. There is no need to search for a root, as no (positive) root exists! As a safety check I verify that the Z difference at this lower bound is positive; otherwise the lower bound is bad. I have never seen this fail.

Finally, we just step forward along the viewing ray in a loop, incrementing t by a tiny amount each time until the Z difference is no longer positive. This will be the first intersection of the ray with the vortex boundary, the one that is seen. To approximate the root I just use the average of the two bounding values. A fanatic would use interpolation, but we are working at such high resolution here that this would be extreme overkill. If, for the sake of speed, you make larger jumps you might want to interpolate. However, jumps large enough to benefit from interpolation might risk skipping over the smallest root. Be careful.

By the way, if anyone comes up with a more clever way to find the smallest root, please send me an email. I'd love to know about it.

Assigning Tones to the Image

At this point we know how to locate the (X, Y, Z) coordinates of every visible point on the vortex that corresponds to a (*Row, Col*) pixel in the viewing window. But what do we do with this information? How do we use it to define the appearance of this pixel? In this presentation I will stick strictly with two tones: black and white. However, I will present sufficient tools for the user to employ fancier ideas, including 24-bit full color.

Computing the Arc Length From the Vortex Center

A key component of visually pleasing and realistic coloring is knowing how far (as the ant crawls) any point on the vortex boundary is from the bottom center of the vortex. This is not the linear (Euclidean) distance. Rather, this is the distance along the profile curve of the vortex. Imagine a tiny insect starting at the very bottom of the vortex, where $X=Y=Radius=0$, and crawling along the vortex boundary until it reaches the point in question. How far did it crawl? Using this distance to assign tones results in a visually pleasing illusion, with perspective and viewing angle giving the impression of realistic depth changes.

The easiest way to compute this distance is with basic numerical integration. We divide the range of the radius, 0 to 1, into a large number of equally spaced intervals. We evaluate the boundary curve at each point and use the Pythagorean theorem to compute a linear approximation to the curve length separating each very closely spaced pair of points. Then we just compute the cumulative sum starting with *Radius*=0. As long as the resolution is fine this produces accurate results.

One caveat is that this is an expensive operation, so we would not want to have to do it for every pixel in the window. Instead we do it just once and place the results in a table, and then use fast binary search to locate entries in the table. The relatively simple code for creating this table appears on the next page, and an explanation appears in comments. We should make the calling parameter length quite large to ensure accuracy. This has negligible effect on speed. We keep this length and the table in static areas for quick access when needed.

```
static int table_length ;
static double *arc_radius, *arc_length ;

int make_arc_table (
   int length  // Length of table; larger makes more accuracy
   )
{
   int i ;
   double eps, value ;

   table_length = length ;
   arc_radius = (double *) malloc ( table_length * sizeof(double) ) ;
   arc_length = (double *) malloc ( table_length * sizeof(double) ) ;

   eps = 1.0 / (table_length - 1.0) ;    // Radius increment separating entries

   for (i=0 ; i<table_length ; i++) {    // Set radius entries and initialize length entries
      arc_radius[i] = i * eps ;          // Radius runs from 0 through 1
      arc_length[i] = curve ( arc_radius[i] ) ; // curve() runs from -1 through 0
      }

   // Pythagorean base is eps and height is arc_length[i] - arc_length[i-1].
   // We must generate the table backwards because we are changing it in place.
   // When this loop is done it contains the lengths of the individual segments.

   for (i=table_length-1 ; i>0 ; i--) {
      value = arc_length[i] - arc_length[i-1] ;          // Height of triangle
      arc_length[i] = sqrt ( eps * eps + value * value ) ; // Pythagorean theorem
      }

   arc_length[0] = 0.0 ;  // By definition

   for (i=1 ; i<table_length ; i++)           // Cumulate individual segments
      arc_length[i] += arc_length[i-1] ;      // i=1 here is redundant but clear

   // Finally we normalize it so that the length ranges from 0 through 1
   for (i=1 ; i<table_length ; i++)  // Normalize to unit total
      arc_length[i] /= arc_length[table_length-1] ;

   return 0 ;  // Actual code contains check for malloc() failure and has error return code
}
```

When we want to compute the length along the arc from the base to a point we must do it in two steps. First we compute the radius at that point; recall that the vortex is circularly symmetric around the Z axis, so the length depends only on the radius, not the individual X and Y values. Then we use the radius to look up the arc length in the precomputed table. The searching code is shown below, and the embedded comments should make it self-explanatory.

```
int search_arc_table ( double radius )
{
   int klo, khi, k ;

/*
   Use binary search to bound radius between klo and khi.
   This binary search algorithm assumes that the value being bounded
   cannot lie below the lowest entry.
   Both of these arrays range from 0 to 1, inclusive.
*/

   if (radius >= arc_radius[table_length-1])  // Outside range means last case
      k = table_length - 1 ;
   else {                        // We need to do binary search
      klo = 0 ;                  // Will have arc_radius[klo] <= radius < arc_radius[khi]
      khi = table_length - 1 ;

      while (khi > klo+1) {     // While not bounded between adjacent table entries
         k = (khi + klo) / 2 ;
         if (radius < arc_radius[k])
            khi = k ;
         else
            klo = k ;
      }
      k = klo ;
   }
   return k ;
}
```

We can put it all together with a simple routine that, given the eye, the window pixel, and the *t* at the vortex intersection, computes the arc length from the vortex base to the point corresponding to *t*. This routine also returns the *X* and *Y* coordinates of the point, as these will likely be needed later to compute the rotational position of the point. Here is this code:

```
double arc_length_from_t (
   double y_eye ,        // <= 0
   double z_eye ,        // > 1
   double row ,          // Row location in view window
   double col ,          // And column
   double t ,            // Relative length of projected ray
   double *x_terminus ,  // Returned X coordinate of intersection
   double *y_terminus    // Returned Y coordinate of intersection
   )
{
   int k ;
   double theta, x_window, y_window, x_delta, y_delta, radius ;

/*
   Find the (X,Y) location of this point exactly as we did earlier
*/

   theta = atan2 ( z_eye , -y_eye ) ;  // Equation (2.6) on Page 16
   x_window = col ;                    // Equation (2.7)
   y_window = row * sin ( theta ) ;    // Equation (2.8)

   x_delta = x_window ;                // Equation (2.4)
   y_delta = y_window - y_eye ;

   *x_terminus = t * x_delta ;         // Equation (2.5)
   *y_terminus = t * y_delta + y_eye ;

   radius = sqrt ( *x_terminus * *x_terminus + *y_terminus * *y_terminus ) ;
   k = search_arc_table ( radius ) ;
   return arc_length[k] ;
}
```

Producing a Checkerboard Vortex

At this point we have all of the tools we need to intelligently color the pixels in the view window. The simplest and (to me) most effective illusion is based on a simple checkerboard in which black and white alternate according to arc length from the base and rotational position. Here is that code. Note that we get the eye position from a global structure vortex_params. This returns the value 1 for white and 0 for black.

```
double compute_checker (
    double row ,     // Row location in view window
    double col       // And column
    )
{
    double t, arc_len ;
    double x_terminus, y_terminus, radius ;
    double tone_from_length, tone_from_angle, final_tone ;

    t = find_t ( vortex_params.eye_Y , vortex_params.eye_Z , row , col ) ;

    if (t > 1.e50)     // Above horizon?
        return 1.0 ;   // Call it white (arbitrary but sensible)

    arc_len = arc_length_from_t ( vortex_params.eye_Y , vortex_params.eye_Z ,
                        row , col , t , &x_terminus , &y_terminus ) ;

    tone_from_length = ((int) (vortex_params.length_divisions * arc_len)) % 2 ;

    tone_from_angle = (atan2 ( x_terminus , y_terminus ) + PI) / (2.0 * PI) ; // Scale it 0-1
    tone_from_angle = ((int)(vortex_params.angle_divisions*tone_from_angle + 0.5)) % 2;

    final_tone = ((int) tone_from_length + (int) (tone_from_angle)) % 2 ; // XOR

    // Make an optional black border
    radius = x_terminus * x_terminus + y_terminus * y_terminus ;
    if (radius >= 1.0 + vortex_params.perim_width)
        final_tone = 1.0 ;       // Vortex is surrounded by white
    else if (radius >= 1.0)     // Except for an optional narrow band of black to define it
        final_tone = 0.0 ;

    return final_tone ;
}
```

Producing a Spiral Vortex

I had hopes that a spiral pattern would be even more impressive than a checkerboard, but I have to admit being disappointed. Nonetheless, here is my attempt at spiral code.

```
double compute_spiral (
   double row ,      // Row location in view window
   double col        // And column
   )
{
   double t, arc_len ;
   double x_terminus, y_terminus, radius, final_tone ;
   double angle_part, length_part ;

   t = find_t ( vortex_params.eye_Y , vortex_params.eye_Z , row , col ) ;

   if (t > 1.e50)  // Above horizon?
     return 1.0 ;

   arc_len = arc_length_from_t ( vortex_params.eye_Y , vortex_params.eye_Z ,
                        row , col , t , &x_terminus , &y_terminus ) ;

   length_part = vortex_params.length_divisions * arc_len ;

/*
   Compute the tone based on rotational position on the vortex
*/
   angle_part = (atan2 ( x_terminus , y_terminus ) + PI) / (2.0 * PI) ;  // Scale it 0-1
   angle_part = vortex_params.angle_divisions * angle_part ;

   final_tone = ((int) (length_part + angle_part)) % 2 ;

   // Make an optional black border
   radius = x_terminus * x_terminus + y_terminus * y_terminus ;
   if (radius >= 1.0 + vortex_params.perim_width)
     final_tone = 1.0 ;
   else if (radius >= 1.0)
     final_tone = 0.0 ;

   return final_tone ;
}
```

The VORTEX Program

When you click the Image / Compute vortex image menu item, the following dialog box appears:

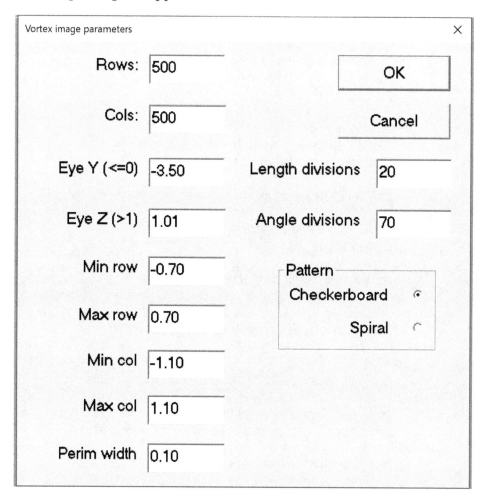

The user specifies the row/column resolution, the eye position (Y<=0; Z>1), the row and column range for the view window, the width of a black perimeter surrounding the vortex, the repeat rate for the pattern for both arc length and rotational position, and the pattern. Under the File menu, any selected image can be printed or saved to a BMP file.

The Blocks Illusion

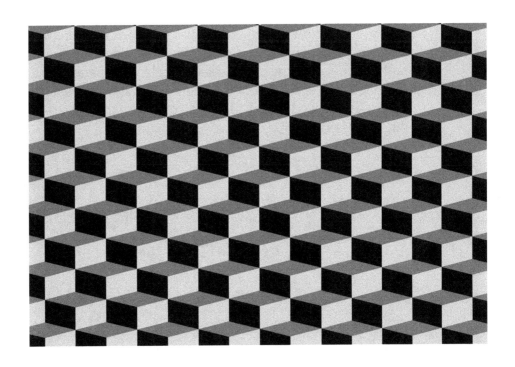

One of the oldest and most common illusions is an array of side-lit blocks that can pop in and out depending on how the viewer perceives them. Perhaps you have seen gorgeous wood inlay productions of this illusion, which is easier to do than one might think. This relative simplicity is due to the fact that only three different shapes, each distinctly colored, are needed. If the craftsperson has the ability to quickly produce a large number of identical copies, such as with a laser cutter or a saw jig, it's just a matter of assembling them carefully using ultimately hidden guidelines. Or, if you have a laser engraver, you can use a standard graphics program to convert the intermediate gray level to a fine scattered dot pattern.

There are only four easily understood parameters that control the three parallelogram shapes (the front, side, and top). These are the height, width, and depth of the block, and the angle that is related to the elevation of the view. This is illustrated in Figure 3.1 below. When the position of a block is referenced in the code, it will reference the front-right-top corner of the block as shown.

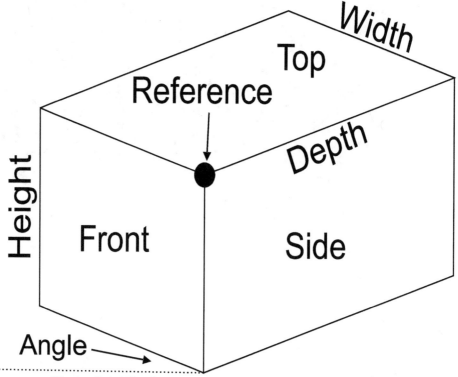

Figure 3.1: The four parameters that define the shapes

The three parallelograms are always assembled as shown in Figure 3.1 to make up a single block unit. These block units are then tiled across the image in a skewed checkerboard pattern. There are only two different matings needed to do this tiling, and they are shown in Figure 3.2. This figure also shows the reference points on each block, so the row and column offset for this mating is the difference between these points.

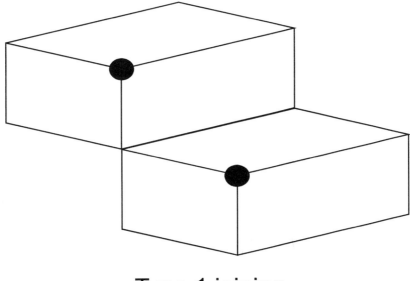

Type 1 joining

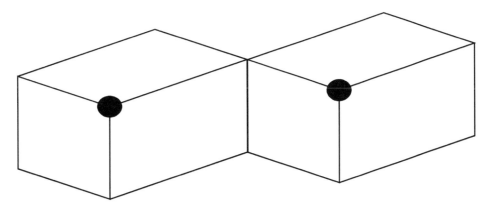

Type 2 joining
Figure 3.2: The two types of block joining for tiling

I have a subroutine that is given the (Row, Column) coordinates of the reference point and draws a single block. The three dimensions of the block, as well as the angle, are retrieved by this subroutine from a global user-parameter structure. This subroutine also returns the row and column differences between adjacent reference points for each of the two joining types.

To tile the blocks in the image, a single block is drawn with its reference point at the center of the image. Then, an 'outer' loop moves one jump at a time in the Type 2 direction to the right or left (separately). For each position, an 'inner' loop places blocks in the Type 1 direction. I do each of the 4 'quadrants' separately, although two inner loop quadrants could be combined in one outer loop. I originally intended to use a sophisticated algorithm to know exactly when to stop placing blocks, so as to avoid wasting computer time, and this algorithm would have required such separation. But when I saw that a ridiculously naive algorithm that does a huge amount of excessive computation still runs in a second or two I abandoned this ambitious algorithm and just over-computed. This pattern of filling is shown in Figure 3.3 below.

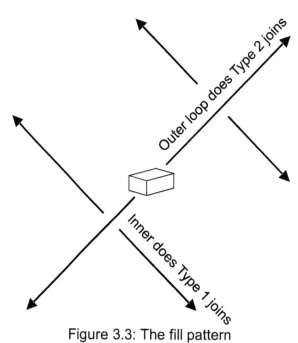

Figure 3.3: The fill pattern

If you modify this code to be more efficient (and thereby save half a second of computer time!), beware of one tricky issue that severely complicates the filling. Suppose you are going up and to the right in the outer loop and going up and to the left in the inner loop. In order to fill in blocks near the upper-right corner of the image, you may have to do many outer-loop 'placements' that are far outside the image, and then many more Type 1 placements that are also outside the image before you get back inside the image! I take the extremely inefficient approach of just doing a huge number of extra placements. Even then, some extreme (and not at all practical) parameter sets may cause incomplete filling.

Numerical issues cause some isolated pixels here and there to remain unset, so the final step in the algorithm is to pass through the entire image and fix this problem.

The complete computer code for this program is in the BLOCKS directory, and the core computations are in COMPUTE.CPP. I won't bother discussing the code here, as it is more fussy than difficult, and the embedded comments should be sufficient for understanding.

The BLOCKS Program

The BLOCKS program lets the user create blcoks images, print them, and save them to disk as BMP files. The main dialog looks like this:

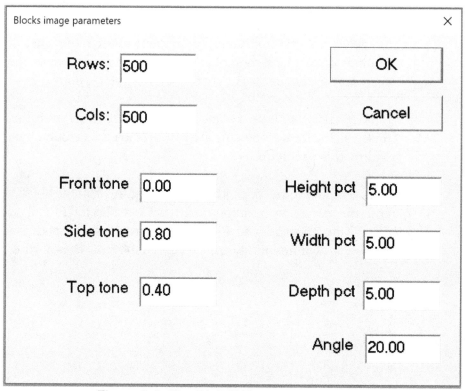

Figure 3.4: The BLOCKS parameter dialog

The image size (resolution) is specified in the *Rows* and *Cols*. The gray levels of the three visible faces are specified in a range from 0 (black) to 1 (254, essentially full white). The edge dimensions are specified as a percentage of the image size. Finally, the angle is specified in degrees and should be limited to reasonable values.

4

Mandelbrot and Julia Sets

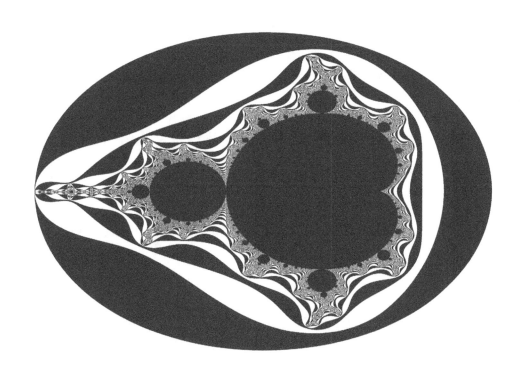

Around the 1980s, once personal computers were available to the masses, amateur and professional programmers everywhere became enthralled with a particular family of patterns called Mandelbrot and Julia sets. I was one of those programmers. Along with about a hundred thousand other people, I wrote and made publicly available a program for computing and displaying images from this family. Mine was better than some others, and weaker than some others, but it sure did produce pretty pictures.

After a few years I put it aside, instead pursuing more montetary-based projects. But when I recently decided to write a book on computer art, I had to dig it out of long-forgotten archives. The original program was written for a 16-bit DOS environment, so I needed to do a massive rewrite to bring it up to a 64-bit Windows environment. I also added a display mode amenable to decorative laser engraving. And so was born JULIA 1.0.

Mathematics of the Mandelbrot Set

This is not an appropriate forum for an in-depth examination of the mathematics of Mandelbrot and Julia sets. In my opinion, the single best reference for those who wish to dig deeper is "The Science of Fractal Images" by Heinz-Otto Peitgen and Dietmar Saupe. Between that book and its extensive bibliography, you will find enough material to fill the remainder of your life.

Complex-Domain Mathematics

Although it may not make much sense to the uninitiated, many branches of mathematics and the sciences find great use for the square root of –1, an imaginary number abbreviated as i. In the complex domain, every 'number' is represented by a real part and an imaginary part, with the imaginary part being the i term. For example, $3+5i$ is a number in the complex domain. As long as we remember that $i^2=-1$, basic math rules hold. For example, $(a+bi)(c+di)=ac-bd+(ad+bc)i$. The absolute value of $a+bi$ is defined as $sqrt(a^2+b^2)$.

The Mandelbrot Set

Consider a sequence of complex numbers. The first member of this sequence is zero. Subsequent members are computed by squaring the prior member, and then adding a complex-domain constant. This sequence is formally defined as follows:

$$Z_0 = 0$$
$$Z_{i+1} = Z_i^2 + c$$

We are now concerned with how this sequence behaves for different values of c. Clearly, if c=0 this sequence is identically zero. Almost as clearly, if c has a large absolute value this series blows up without bound. *The Mandelbrot set is defined as the set of all complex numbers c such that this sequence does not blow up, but rather remains bounded forever.* So if we want to see if a particular constant c is a member of the Mandelbrot set, all we have to do is iterate as shown above, and if we are able to perform an infinite number of iterations without the series blowing up, we have the answer. Simple, right?

Well, not quite so simple. An algorithm which requires an infinite number of iterations to check whether the sequence ever attains infinite value would consume an infinite amount of computer time; that's not practical. We are partially rescued by a theorem from complex mathematics. It states that the above sequence will remain bounded if and only if its absolute value never exceeds two. We therefore know that we can stop iterating as soon as we get a value whose absolute value exceeds two; we don't have to wait for it to reach infinity. The 'c' for such a sequence is not in the Mandelbrot set.

But that solves only half of the problem. How long do we need to continue when the sequence *appears* to remain bounded? Who is to say that it won't remain bounded for millions of iterations, without ever passing two, and then suddenly explode toward infinity? This can happen, but much experience has shown it to be so rare that a simple and inexpensive precaution is sufficient for us to ignore the possibility.

All we have to do is set an upper limit on the number of times the iteration will be done, and make sure this *Dwell Limit* is reasonably large. Setting an appropriate value will be discussed later. Our assumption is that if a large number of members of the sequence have been computed and we haven't passed an absolute value of 2 yet, then it's reasonably certain that we never will. It should be obvious that the Dwell Limit involves a tradeoff between speed and quality. A large Dwell Limit will burn a lot of computer time for values of c in the Mandelbrot set, because we'll keep iterating right up to that limit. But if we set the Dwell Limit too small we will sometimes give up too quickly, deciding that the trial c is a member of the Mandelbrot set when in fact it is not.

The *dwell* of a value of c which lies outside the Mandelbrot set is defined as the number of iterations which were required before the decision to exclude it from the set was made. This decision is typically based on comparing its absolute value to two. But a good program will give the user the option of setting this *Escape Constant* to any value of at least two. Obviously, any escape constant of at least two will, given a sufficient number of iterations, lead to the same decision. The only effect is that larger escape constants will require more iterations to make the decision. This is why we typically use two; it is the smallest such constant and hence will require the fewest iterations to reach a decision.

A good way to display the Mandelbrot set is to plot it as a graphic in which the horizontal axis is the real part of the constant c, and the vertical axis is the imaginary part. This is done in the plot shown on the title page of this chapter. Strictly speaking, this plot would be binary, perhaps with all members of the Mandelbrot set colored black and other points being white. However, the dwell of each point can be used to enhance the visual display of the set. In a manner of speaking, the dwell can be considered to be related to the 'distance' from the point to the Mandelbrot set. If the dwell is small then the sequence blew up fast, so the point is far away. On the other hand, points with a dwell very near the Dwell Limit may be said to be very near the set. Later we will see how the dwell can be used to reveal much more information than a simple binary map.

One other consideration in display of Mandelbrot sets is the fact that the angle of the final point in the series can sometimes be of interest. (Actually, that 'angle' description is close but not quite correct; the exact definition is beyond the scope of this book. See Section 4.2.6 of "The Science of Fractal Images" for full details.) My *JULIA* program takes a simplified but effective approach to this display modification, using the sign of the imaginary component of the last point to determine the low-order bit of the point's dwell. More details will appear in the code and example sections.

Julia Sets

In the prior section we saw that membership in the Mandelbrot set can be determined by iterating a simple equation: just square the prior iterate and add a constant. The iteration always begins at 0, and the point corresponding to the constant does or does not belong to the Mandelbrot set according to whether the iteration blows up or remains trapped within a radius of two.

The *Julia set* reverses the roles of the starting point and the constant. The additive constant is fixed and defines the nature of the Julia set; every constant corresponds to a different Julia set, with some constants not even corresponding to a Julia set. A point is classified as belonging or not belonging to the Julia set by starting the iteration with that point and seeing if the iteration blows up or remains confined to within a radius of two.

Dwell Computation with the Definition Algorithm

There are two methods used by JULIA to speed the process of deciding whether or not a point lies in the set. These methods often let us decide that a point is a member of the set without having to process the entire Dwell Limit iterations.

One method is to check to see if we have arrived at a fixed point. There are many locations inside the set that are attractive (not just in the sense of being pretty!). In other words, such points act as traps, sucking iterates into their 'gravitational field' until the iterates spiral into the fixed point, and then holding the iterates there forever. If two successive iterates are equal then all iterates from that time on will be equal. Since we are working with a finite-precision machine, it is necessary to slightly modify this test. We only ask for equality relative to floating point precision. Fanatics may also verify that their absolute value is not close to 2, as then it is reasonably safe to assume that the sequence is converging to a fixed point safely inside the set. However, I find that the check for nearness to 2 to be overkill.

The second test is for periodic sequences. We just saw that single points can be attractive fixed points. It is also possible for closed loops to be attractive. There are an infinite number of points inside the set for which the sequence endlessly repeats the same subsequence. If we have done a lot of iterations, are still not near an absolute value of 2, but also are not converging on a fixed point, then a lot of time can be saved if this periodic behavior can be discovered. The simple minded approach would be to save each iterate as it is computed. Then after computing the next, compare it to all previous iterates. If a match happens even once then a periodic subsequence has been found. But there is a clever and much more thrifty alternative.

An efficient way to check for periodic behavior is to first let some iterations pass, to avoid wasting time checking for periodic behavior that has not started yet; exactly how many is fairly arbitrary and not terribly critical. Then begin saving points. For each point, see if it is equal (to machine precision) to a prior point, but advance the prior point only every *two* iterations. For example, you might compare points 101 and 102 with point

100, 103 and 104 with 101, 105 and 106 with 102, and so forth. This successively increases the period being sought. If we start too late and miss the period it's no problem because this will catch any integer multiple of the period. So every possible period length is checked, but with only one compare per iteration. Slightly more sophistication is possible but overkill (in my opinion).

Here is the algorithm implemented in *JULIA* for computing the number of iterations (the *dwell*) before either reaching the Dwell Limit and concluding that the point is in the Mandelbrot or Julia set, or reaching the Escape Radius and concluding that it is not. The two shortcuts just discussed are included. C++ source code for this routine is in COUNTIT.CPP. The following items must be supplied:

LOOP_TEST_START - The number of iterations before beginning the loop test. I use 50, but the exact value is not critical.

LOOP_TEST_END - The number of iterations before giving up on the loop test. I use 2000, but the exact value is not critical.

DwellLimit - Stop iterating after this many iterations.

EscapeConstant - Stop iterating if an iterate exceeds this value.

COMPLEX c - Constant in iteration $Z(k+1) = Z(k)^2 + c$

COMPLEX *z_start - Starting point of iteration

COMPLEX loop_work - Work area DwellLimit long

Note... For Julia sets, **c** defines the particular set and **z_start** is the location on the plane being evaluated for membership. For Mandelbrot, **c** is the location in the plane being evaluated for membership, and the starting Z for iteration is 0. But when this is called for Mandelbrot, we might as well start the iteration at **c** because if we start at 0 the next Z will be **c**. This saves a single iteration. Waste not, want not. Note that this inconsequentially impacts the DwellLimit test in the algorithm below.

z = z_start
count = 0
loop_index = 0

Begin loop:

    If absval (z) > EscapeConstant   *This point is not in the set*
       Break out of loop

    count = count + 1
    If count = DwellLimit   *This point is in the set*
       Break out of loop   *Breaks one too soon for Julia; no big deal*

    next_z = z^2 + c   *The next iterate*

    Occasionally check for convergence to fixed point; 50 is arbitrary

    If count mod 50 = 0 AND absval (next_z - z) is tiny relative to z
       count = DwellLimit
       Break out of loop

    If count gets to LOOP starting limit, commence loop test

    If count >= LOOP_TEST_START AND count <= LOOP_TEST_END)
       If count > LOOP_TEST_START *Ensure first element is defined*
      AND absval (next_z - loop_work[(count-LOOP_TEST_START)/2])
         is tiny relative to next_z
        count = DwellLimit
        Break out of loop
      loop_work[loop_index] = next_z
      loop_index = loop_index + 1

    z = next_z

End loop

return count (the dwell of this point) and z (for use in angle display)

Binary Maps with the MSETDIST Algorithm

The 'definitional' algorithm just shown has the advantage of not only categorizing points as members or nonmembers of the Mandelbrot/Julia set, but in addition, for nonmembers it provides the dwell, the number of iterations before the series passed the Escape Radius. This provides an additional dimension to work with, as using the dwell to control brightness and/or color can produce dramatic and informative images.

However, this algorithm does not do a very good job of producing visually pleasing *binary* member/nonmember images. Technically, the algorithm is correct in the sense that as long as the Dwell Limit is large enough, each point is correctly classified as a member or nonmember of the set. The problem is that in 'busy' areas, which are the rule at high magnification, the image becomes perforated: in a large fraction of the image, adjacent pixels are opposite classes. In other words, one pixel may be a member, its neighbor a non-member, the next neighbor a member, and so forth. This gives rise to a salt-and-pepper display that looks blurred and almost random. Such images are not usually pretty.

There is an alternative algorithm, called MSETDIST in *The Science of Fractal Images*, which solves this problem, though without providing dwell information. Nonetheless, if your goal is a high-contrast black-and-white image, which for example would be the case with using a laser engraver to burn the image onto a workpiece, the MSETDIST algorithm is ideal.

This algorithm does not classify points as members or nonmembers. Rather, for any given point, the algorithm computes the distance separating that point from the *nearest* point that is a member of the Mandelbrot/Julia set. Of course, if the point under consideration is a member of the set, the computed distance will be zero. But for points outside the set, this computed distance can be used as a threshold for displaying the point as a member or nonmember. This 'fudge factor' can greatly reduce or eliminate the ugly salt-and-pepper effect while still clearly portraying the outline of the set. For example, if we set a distance threshold of 1.5 pixels, alternating membership will be not be displayed; any point within 1.5 pixels of the set will be classified as a member.

The theoretical underpinnings of the MSETDIST algorithm are far beyond the scope of this book; see Section 4.2.5 and the next few pages of *The Science of Fractal Images* for details. The bottom line is that we set an Escape Radius *much* larger than the usual 2.0. We also set a very large Dwell Limit; if in a high magnification area that contains a lot of detail, I often use as much as 100,000 or more. The authors of that book state that the quality and appearance of the image are strongly dependent on these values. However, I have always found that as long as both are set extremely large, all is good. The dependence on these parameters happens only when they are too small. In my experience they cannot be too large, but they can definitely be too small. If in doubt, make them bigger!

For both Mandelbrot and Julia sets, we iterate with the usual equation and starting conditions:

$$Z_{i+1} = Z_i^2 + c \qquad (4.1)$$

For the Mandelbrot set we start the iteration at $Z_0=0$ and vary c. For the Julia set we fix c and vary the starting point. Every iterate should be saved. If we reach the Dwell Limit without exceeding the Escape Radius we are in the set and hence return a distance of zero. Nothing more needs to be done for this tested point.

As we perform those iterations, we also need to compute and save the first derivative of Z_i with respect to the complex-valued point p being tested for membership. We abbreviate this gradient as $Z_i'=dZ_i/dp$. The gradient is slightly different for Mandelbrot (Equation (4.2)) and Julia (Equation (4.3)) sets. Both are easy to compute. They could be computed as we go, but it is slightly faster to compute Equation (4.1) until either the Escape Radius is exceeded or the Dwell Limit is reached, saving the results, and then computing the derivatives from the saved results only if needed.

$$Z_{i+1}' = 2 Z_i Z_i' + 1 \ , \quad Z_0' = 0 \quad \textit{(Mandelbrot)} \quad (4.2)$$

$$Z_{i+1}' = 2 Z_i Z_i' \ , \quad Z_0' = 1 \quad \textit{(Julia)} \qquad (4.3)$$

If we pass the Escape Radius before reaching the Dwell Limit, we can compute a fairly tight upper bound for the distance between the tested point and the nearest point in the set via Equation (4.4), in which Z_n is the last iterate, the one in which we passed the Escape Radius.

$$Distance \le \frac{|Z_n|}{|Z_n'|} \log|Z_n|$$ (4.4)

Here is the MSETDIST algorithm. Source code is in MSETDIST.CPP. The following items must be supplied by the caller:

LARGE - A very large number, typically 1000-10,000 or so
COMPLEX *c - The c parameter in Equation (4.1)
COMPLEX *start - The iteration starting value
max_dwell - Dwell Limit, should be as large as practical
julia - Logical: Is this a Julia set? (versus Mandelbrot)
COMPLEX orbit - Work area max_dwell long

```
iter = 0 ;
z = start

Begin loop
  orbit[iter] = z
  If absval (z) > LARGE      This point is not in the set
    Break out of loop
  z = z^2 + c                The next iterate
  iter = iter + 1
  If iter > max_dwell
    Break out of loop
End loop

If absval (z) > LARGE        Not in the set?
  deriv = 1.0   Recall when called for Mandelbrot, starts at c not 0
  i = 0
  Begin loop
    If i = iter
      Break out of loop
    Compute next_deriv as gradient at iter i+1
    next_deriv = 2 * orbit[i] * deriv        Equation (4.3)
    If ! julia
      next_deriv = next_deriv + 1            Equation (4.2)
    If absval (next_deriv ) > 1.e30
      return 0.0 ;
    deriv = next_deriv
    i = i + 1
  End loop
  return 2 * log ( absval(z) ) * absval ( z ) / absval ( deriv )     Eq (4.4)
return 0.0 ;
```

A few things need to be said about the algorithm just shown. Most important, understand that *officially* the Mandelbrot iteration starts at $z=0$, but I don't in my code. The next iterate would be c (look at Equation (4.1), so I start there, which saves one iteration and slightly simplifies the MSETDIST code. Technically, this changes the meaning of the Dwell Limit (max_dwell) by one for Mandelbrot versus Julia sets, a fact that is utterly inconsequential.

The Escape Radius is typically 2 with the dwell counting method shown in the prior section, because once the iteration passes 2 it blows up rapidly. Thus, using 2 as the Escape Radius minimizes the number of iterations required and hence speeds computation. However, the MSETDIST algorithm requires a lot of iterations in order to produce a good approximation to the distance. Thus we are inclined to set the Escape Radius (LARGE here) to a much larger number, certainly at least several hundred, and preferably somewhat larger if computer time allows. In my code I hard-code 100,000 as the square of the Escape Radius.

If we break out of this large Escape Radius before hitting the Dwell Limit we are not in the set. In this case, use Equation (4.2) or (4.3) iteratively, employing the saved iterates. Alert readers may note that the Mandelbrot derivative iteration *officially* starts at 0, while the Julia starts at 1. Yet the algorithm just shown starts at 1 regardless of the set type. This is because, as stated a moment ago, I start the Mandelbrot iteration at c rather than at 0. The derivative in this case is 1, the same as for Julia sets.

Finally, we break out of the derivative loop if the next derivative is gigantic. It will continue blowing up if this happens, so we might as well quit. A glance at Equation (4.4) tells us that in this case the distance will be so close to 0 that we might as well call it 0.

Calling the Dwell and MSETDIST Algorithms

I'm going to show a C++ code fragment (from EXECUTE.CPP) just to make completely clear the way that the two algorithms just shown would typically be called. Naturally, feel free to modify the code as you wish; this is just a template for clarity. Here is the code; a discussion follows.

```
real_inc = (MaxR - MinR) / (ColResolution - 1) ;
imag_inc = (MinI - MaxI) / (RowResolution - 1) ;

for (irow=0 ; irow<RowResolution ; irow++) {
  dwell_ptr = dwells + irow * ColResolution ;
  z_start.imag = MaxI + imag_inc * (double) irow ;
  for (icol=0 ; icol<ColResolution ; icol++) {
    z_start.real = MinR + real_inc * (double) icol ;
    if (DwellVsBinary) {      // Dwell method
      if (ObjectType == 2)    // Julia
        *dwell_ptr++ = countit ( &c_param , &z_start , &end , loop_real, loop_imag ) ;
      else                    // Mandelbrot
        *dwell_ptr++ = countit ( &z_start , &z_start , &end, loop_real, loop_imag) ;
      if (BinaryDecomp  &&  (*(dwell_ptr-1) < DwellLimit)) { // See page 39
        *(dwell_ptr-1) &= 0xFFFFFFFE ;  // This assumes dwell is four bytes
        if (end.imag  >  0.0)
          ++*(dwell_ptr-1) ;
      }
    }

    else {                    // MSETDIST binary map method
      delta = BinaryThreshold * 0.5 * (real_inc - imag_inc) ;
      if (ObjectType == 2) // Julia
        *dwell_ptr++ = msetdist (
                      &c_param, &z_start, DwellLimit, 1, lp_real, lp_imag ) < delta ;
      else
        *dwell_ptr++ = msetdist (
                      &z_start, &z_start, DwellLimit, 0, lp_real , lp_imag ) < delta ;
    }
  } // For all cols
} // For all rows
```

MaxR, MinR, MaxI, MinI are the limits over which the set points will be processed, with the real axis being horizontal (increasing to the right) and the imaginary axis being vertical (increasing upward). RowResolution and ColResolution are the number of rows and columns in the computed image. We first compute the real and imaginary increments between columns and rows. Note that the imaginary increment will be negative.

The outermost loop passes through the rows, one at a time, with the maximum imaginary value going in the top row and working downward from there. Then the inner loop passes across the columns of a row, left to right.

The flag DwellVsBinary holds the user's choice of whether we will use the definitional algorithm (in COUNTIT.CPP), which provides dwells, or the MSETDIST algorithm, which provides binary inclusion flags.

In both countit() and msetdist() the first calling parameter is the constant c and the second is the starting point. In the case of Julia sets, these are exactly as expected, where c_param is the Julia parameter c and the point being tested defines the starting point for the iteration. For Mandelbrot sets, things may appear a bit funny at first glance. Recall that the c parameter is defined by the point being tested, and we officially start the iteration at zero. But since the result of the first iteration is the c parameter, I start iteration there to save one iteration (trivia) and slightly simplify the MSETDIST code (almost trivia). Thus, in this code I set both parameters equal to each other, the tested point (z_start).

If the user has selected the dwell method and has also specified that binary decomposition be used for the display, we zero out the low-order bit of the dwell and then set it according to the sign of the imaginary part of the final iterate. This display option was discussed on Page 39.

Mandelbrot and Julia Sets in the Quaternion Domain

Every number in the complex domain that we have been considering has two parts, one real and one imaginary (*i*). This concept can be usefully extended to the *quaterion domain*, in which every number has four parts, one real and three imaginary (*i*, *j*, *k*). The quaterion domain has enormous utility in various practical applications, including analysis of radar returns and four-dimensional object tracking (three physical dimensions plus time). Such applications are far beyond the scope of this book; here we will explore how Mandelbrot and Julia sets can exist in the quaternion domain.

The most obvious problem we'll face in this endeavor is how to display an object that exists in the quaternion domain. It's hard enough displaying a three-dimensional object on a two-dimensional surface such as a computer screen or piece of paper. A four-dimensional object would seem impossible to display.

The method we will use is to take a cross section of the object, thus reducing its dimension by 1, from 4 to 3. To understand this, think for a moment about slicing an apple (a 3D object) and examining the exposed surface (a 2D view). Depending on the direction and position of the slicing operation, you may see circular symmetry (if the stem was pointed directly at you), or the seeds and core in a line (if the stem was pointed to a side) or any of an infinite number of other possible patterns.

Of course we could slice a quaternion object twice, reducing it to two dimensions and hence directly displayable. But it's far more interesting to slice just once, creating a 3D object, and then use ray tracing to display that object. This is the approach used in *JULIA*.

Quaternion Mathematics

A quaternion number may be represented as a + b*i* + c*j* + d*k*. Addition of two quaternions is exactly as would be expected, with each of the four parts added separately. However, multiplication is more complicated, being governed by the following rules:

1) $i * i = j * j = k * k = -1$
2) $i * j = k$; $j * k = i$; $k * i = j$
3) $j * i = -k$; $k * j = -i$; $i * k = -j$

Note from the second and third rule sets that multiplication is not commutative.

Step 1 of 2: Locate Intersections of Eye Ray with Object

This and the next section assume that the reader has at least a basic understanding of ray tracing, so I will simply summarize the actions of the algorithms, all of which can be found in QUATERN.CPP.

We begin with an overview of the grand scheme. The 4-dimensional object lies entirely within a hypersphere centered at the origin and with radius 2. The user selects which of the four dimensions (real, i, j, k) to collapse, indicated by an integer 0-3, leaving us with a 3-dimensional profile. Those three dimensions are mapped to the X, Y, and Z axes in the same order as the quaternion dimensions, using a standard right-handed coordinate system. For example, if the user wishes to collapse dimension 2 (the j dimension), the real axis maps to X, the i axis to Y, and the k axis to Z. Thus, we are dealing strictly with a 3-dimensional object; the fourth dimension has been sliced out of existence.

We use orthographic projection, meaning that the eye is at infinity. The user specifies a view direction as Elevation and Azimuth. If both are set to 0 we look at the object from infinitely far out on the +X axis. The Azimuth (0-360 degrees) is counterclockwise rotation around the Z (vertical) axis. The Elevation (0-90 degrees) is the angle that the view direction makes with the XY plane; an elevation of 90 degrees means that we are looking straight down at the object from infinitely far away in the +Z direction.

For each pixel in the view plane (a plane through the origin and perpendicular to the view ray) we consider the *view ray* as being a line passing through that pixel and extending toward the infinitely distant eye. We attempt to find the intersection of the view ray with the object. If there is no intersection (the view ray passes the object without ever touching it) we make note of that fact so that we can later color this pixel black. If there are multiple intersections we find the one that is closest to the eye, as that is the one that would be seen.

This task is performed by tracquat() in QUATERN.CPP. This routine must be provided with several quantities. First, in most cases the user will want the center of the quaternion object to be at the 3D origin, meaning that the center of the object will correspond to the center of the display. But this is not required; the object can be shifted to focus attention on a particular location. The 4D coordinates that will be centered are specified as **Rcent**, **Icent**, **Jcent**, and **Kcent**. They would generally all be zero. Shifting them may not always provide intuitive results due to interactions between the dimension being collapsed and the view angle.

The user also supplies the magnification, **magnif**. This is the reciprocal of the radius around the 4D center that will be displayed. Since the object is enclosed in a sphere of radius 2, the typical magnification is 0.5.

As mentioned earlier, we specify **collapse** as an integer from 0 to 3 to define the dimension that will be collapsed out for slicing.

If we are to display a Julia object we must specify the *c* parameter, **jparam**. If we are displaying a Mandelbrot object this parameter is not needed. It plays no direct role in the ray tracing, only being passed to the core computation routine that will be discussed later.

The viewing eye's elevation, **elev**, and azimuth, **az**, are specified. The algorithm shown soon will compute one complete row of the display. The caller must specify the location of that row on the view plane, **rowpos**, with 0.5 for the top row and –0.5 for the bottom. It will compute **ncols** equally spaced columns. The output values, placed in **out**, will generally range from –2 for the most distant (from the eye) possible point, to +2 for the closest possible, with –10 flagging a miss (no intersection).

Here begins the algorithm, broken into small parts for easy digestion. Setup the coordinates of the left and right ends of this line (row) as if the elevation and azimuth were 0 (ie viewing from +X). We'll fix this later. Also compute the view ray increments, which define the direction of moving toward the object from the eye. Assume for the moment that **collapse**=3, so (X,Y,Z) is (R,I,J). We'll fix that later by reassigning axes if necessary. Under these assumptions, as we scan across columns of the row, the real component (X) will be constantly zero, and the *i* component (Y) will cover the full range of the user-specified magnification. The *j* component (Z, vertical) is determined by the caller-specified row. Finally, since we are looking in from the +X direction, which is the real component, moving along the view line will push us strictly in the real direction, with the other components unchanged as we move.

```
Rleft = Rright = 0. ;     // Looking in from +X (Real), so real is constant
Ileft = - 1. / magnif ;   // I goes across columns of this row
Iright = 1. / magnif ;
Jleft = Jright = 2. * rowpos / magnif ;  // J (vertical, Z) corresponds to row
Kleft = Kright = 0. ;     // Assume for now K collapsed out per user

Rrayinc = -1. ;           // Looking in from +X
Irayinc = Jrayinc = Krayinc = 0. ;
```

The code just shown assumes the azimuth and elevation are both zero. Fix things now to account for the actual user-specified values. This is just basic 3D rotation, explained in nearly any 3D graphics text. In fact, if you remember highschool trigonometry these formulas will make sense.

```
deg_rad = 3.141592653589793 / 180.0

SinEl = sin ( deg_rad * elev )
CosEl = cos ( deg_rad * elev )
SinAz = sin ( deg_rad * az )
CosAz = cos ( deg_rad * az )

// Left end of line (this row)
Xtemp = - Jleft * SinEl    // First we elevate (Recall x=0)
Ytemp = Ileft
Ztemp = Jleft * CosEl
Rleft = Xtemp * CosAz  -  Ytemp * SinAz   // Then we rotate about Z
Ileft = Xtemp * SinAz  +  Ytemp * CosAz
Jleft = Ztemp
```

```
// Right end of line (row)
Xtemp = - Jright * SinEl     // First we elevate (Recall x=0)
Ytemp = Iright
Ztemp = Jright * CosEl
Rright = Xtemp * CosAz  -  Ytemp * SinAz   // Then we rotate about Z
Iright = Xtemp * SinAz  +  Ytemp * CosAz
Jright = Ztemp

// View raw direction from eye to object
Xtemp = Rrayinc * CosEl - Jrayinc * SinEl   // First we elevate
Ytemp = Irayinc
Ztemp = Jrayinc * CosEl + Rrayinc * SinEl
Rrayinc = Xtemp * CosAz  -  Ytemp * SinAz   // Then we rotate about Z
Irayinc = Xtemp * SinAz  +  Ytemp * CosAz
Jrayinc = Ztemp
```

We also assumed that **collapse**=3. If this is not the case we have to swap axes.

```
if (collapse == 0)
   Kleft = Jleft
   Jleft = Ileft
   Ileft = Rleft
   Rleft = 0.
   Kright = Jright
   Jright = Iright
   Iright = Rright
   Rright = 0.
   Krayinc = Jrayinc
   Jrayinc = Irayinc
   Irayinc = Rrayinc
   Rrayinc = 0.

else if (collapse == 1)
   Kleft = Jleft
   Jleft = Ileft
   Ileft = 0.
   Kright = Jright
   Jright = Iright
   Iright = 0.
   Krayinc = Jrayinc
   Jrayinc = Irayinc
   Irayinc = 0.
```

```
else if (collapse == 2)
    Kleft = Jleft
    Jleft = 0.
    Kright = Jright
    Jright = 0.
    Krayinc = Jrayinc
    Jrayinc = 0.
```

The user may have asked for the object to be shifted in 4D space so that its origin is no longer at the 3D origin. This allows focus on a particular area of the object. Shift the center of the object to be the user's chosen center of view.

```
Rleft += Rcent
Ileft += Icent
Jleft += Jcent
Kleft += Kcent
Rright += Rcent
Iright += Icent
Jright += Jcent
Kright += Kcent
```

Compute the tiny 4D vector that will be added to the view point each time we advance one column across the row. Moving from the first image column to the last will move us from the left end of the row to the right end, with this movement being orthogonal to the view ray.

```
Rcolinc = (Rright - Rleft) / (double) (ncols-1)
Icolinc = (Iright - Ileft) / (double) (ncols-1)
Jcolinc = (Jright - Jleft) / (double) (ncols-1)
Kcolinc = (Kright - Kleft) / (double) (ncols-1)
```

This is the main outermost loop that traverses the row, doing one pixel at a time. For each pixel we will move from a point that is just outside the object's enclosing sphere (on the eye side) toward the object, stopping when we get very close to the object. The first time we get very close we call that the intersection point, the point where the view ray touches the object. Since it is the first such intersection, this is the one that the eye would see. If we pass through to the other side of the enclosing sphere without ever getting very close to the object, we flag it as a miss.

How close is 'very close'? That is defined by eps in this code. Recall that the row begins at –1/magnif and ends at +1/magnif, a total distance of 2/magnif. This distance covers ncols pixels, meaning that each pixel accounts for 2/(magnif*ncols). I arbitrarily define 'very close' as one-quarter of a pixel. Change this if you wish, but be warned that this value works well.

```
eps = 0.25 * 2. / (magnif * (double) ncols) ;
```

```
col = 0
Begin column loop
   Rpt = Rleft + col * Rcolinc
   Ipt = Ileft + col * Icolinc
   Jpt = Jleft + col * Jcolinc
   Kpt = Kleft + col * Kcolinc
```

We first need to find the starting point for the search. This is a point on the view ray that is outside the enclosing sphere, but not too far outside (or we will waste computer time traversing unnecessary distance in the real search later). There is an explicit formula for the intersection of a ray and a sphere, but I find it easier to just start well outside and take relatively large jumps until we cross to inside the sphere, and then undo that last bad jump. This naive approach wastes an almost unmeasureably tiny amount of time and is easy to understand.

We start well outside the sphere and then move along the view ray parametrically: *TestPoint = ViewPoint - t * RayIncrement*. We need not consider values of the parameter t outside (-4, 4), although here I set the limits at 4.1 for a margin of safety. Where does the number 4 come from? It would be senseless for the user to specify a view center more than 2 units away from the origin, because the object is confined within a sphere of radius 2 around the origin. If the center were at that extreme, it would take 4 units of t (recall that the length of _rayinc is 1) to get to the opposite side of the containing sphere: 2 to reach the origin, and 2 more to reach the opposite side of the enclosing sphere. Thus we start the search at t=4.1 and assume we have passed right by the sphere (which can happen at large offsets) if t reaches –4.1.

t = 4.1   *Start on the eye side of the sphere*
Begin sphere-seeking loop
   If t < -4.1   *Passed right by the sphere?*
      Break out of sphere-seeking loop

   Define the trial starting point parametrically along view ray

   start.r = Rpt - t * Rrayinc
   start.i = Ipt - t * Irayinc
   start.j = Jpt - t * Jrayinc
   start.k = Kpt - t * Krayinc

   If we are still outside the sphere, move a little closer
   But if we are now inside, undo the last move and quit looking

   If start.r * start.r + start.i * start.i + start.j * start.j + start.k * start.k > 4.4
      t -= 0.5   *Move a little closer to object; .5 is arbitrary*

   Else
      t += 0.5   *Crossed to inside. Go back to prior t and quit.*
      start.r = Rpt - t * Rrayinc
      start.i = Ipt - t * Irayinc
      start.j = Jpt - t * Jrayinc
      start.k = Kpt - t * Krayinc
      Break out of sphere-seeking loop

End sphere-seeking loop

For problematic magnification and center we might miss the sphere.

If t < -4.1
   *out++ = MISS
   Go to the top of the column loop, skipping the refinement code

At this point, **QUATERION start** is a good starting point for a slower, more refined search. It is just slightly outside the bounding sphere, on the eye side. Now we need to keep moving toward the object until we either get very close (**eps**) or pass by or through it.

For this task we will use a slightly modified version of the MSETDIST algorithm presented starting on Page 43. Recall that the algorithm computes a fairly tight upper bound on the distance between a given point and the nearest point in the Mandelbrot/Julia set. The modification we make is to multiply the computed distance by a small value (0.25 in my code). Although it is not absolutely guaranteed, it is for all practical purposes guaranteed that this shrunken distance will be less than the actual distance. Therefore, the algorithm to travel along the view ray until we get very close to the object is simple: compute the (underestimated) distance and move that much closer to the object. Repeat until we are close enough. This algorithm would fail if the computed distance were larger than the actual distance, but by shrinking it we make this possibility rare to the point of being practically impossible.

In the algorithm below, we compare the squared distance of the test point from the origin to 10 (somewhat arbitrary) to see if we passed right by the object without ever getting close enough. We call the MSETDIST algorithm with the same parameters used earlier (discussed starting on Page 43. If the test point is very close to the object we store its parametric parameter t and quit refining. Otherwise we move closer and test again.

```
Begin refinement loop
  If (start.r * start.r + start.i * start.i + start.j * start.j + start.k * start.k >10)
    *out++ = MISS          Passed to other side without hit
    Break out of refinement loop

  if (ObjectType == 4)          Julia quaternion
    dist = msetdist_q ( &start , jparam , DwellLimit , 1 , orbit )
  else if (ObjectType == 3)      Mandelbrot quaternion
    dist = msetdist_q ( &start , &start , DwellLimit , 0 , orbit )

  If (dist < eps)      This point on the ray is effectively on the object
    *out++ = t      We store only t because we can recreate 4D point
    Break out of refinement loop

  Else
    t -= dist ;        // Move a little closer to the object
    start.r = Rpt - t * Rrayinc ;
    start.i = Ipt - t * Irayinc ;
    start.j = Jpt - t * Jrayinc ;
    start.k = Kpt - t * Krayinc ;
End refinement loop
col = col + 1
If col == ncols
  Break out of column loop
End column loop
```

Step 2 of 2: Compute the Image

At this point we have an nrows by ncols matrix quat_dist of t values from tracquat(). The user has specified the magnification, magnif, as well as the type of lighting to use, lighting, with the following possible values:

0 - No lighting; display based on t (diagnostic only, usually ugly)
1 - Single white light at eye (usually best)
2 - RBG staggered around eye
3 - Single white light above object (+Z)
4 - RGB staggered above object (+Z)

The first step is to find the direction of the eye. This will be needed later to determine if a light source is on the same side of a surface of the object as the eye.

```
deg_rad = 3.141592653589793 / 180.0
rhalf = sqrt ( 1. / 2. )
rthird = sqrt ( 1. / 3. )

SinEl = sin ( deg_rad * Elevation )
CosEl = cos ( deg_rad * Elevation )
SinAz = sin ( deg_rad * Azimuth )
CosAz = cos ( deg_rad * Azimuth )

xeye = CosEl * CosAz
yeye = CosEl * SinAz
zeye = SinEl
```

We set the location of the lights. Cases 0 and 1 will be handled individually later, so we don't need to worry about them now.

```
Switch (lighting)
  case 2:              RGB staggered around eye
    Red at (1,0,1)
    RlightX = rhalf * CosAz * (CosEl - SinEl)
    RlighY = rhalf * SinAz * (CosEl - SinEl)
    RlightZ = rhalf * (CosEl + SinEl)

    Green at (1,-1,-1)
    GlightX = rthird * (CosAz * SinEl + CosAz * CosEl + SinAz)
    GlightY = rthird * (SinAz * SinEl + SinAz * CosEl - CosAz)
    GlightZ = rthird * (SinEl - CosEl)
```

Blue at (1,1,-1)
BlightX = rthird * (CosAz * SinEl + CosAz * CosEl - SinAz)
BlightY = rthird * (SinAz * SinEl + SinAz * CosEl + CosAz)
BlightZ = rthird * (SinEl - CosEl)
Break out of switch

case 3:   *White above*
   RlightX = 0.0
   RlightY = 0.0
   RlightZ = 1.0
   Break out of switch

case 4:   *RGB staggered above*
   RlightX = -rhalf
   RlightY = 0.0
   RlightZ = rhalf
   GlightX = rthird
   GlightY = -rthird
   GlightZ = rthird
   BlightX = rthird
   BlightY = rthird
   BlightZ = rthird
   break out of switch

Compute a scaling factor that controls how changes in t map to changes in the distance in the view ray direction. To understand, assume that magnif=1 and nrows=ncols, which we will call n. Recall that traversing the image from top to bottom or left to right is a distance of 2 (–1 to 1). Thus, changing one row or column moves a distance of 2/n units. Equivalently, a unit change is a move of n/2 rows or columns. So factor here multiplies t by n/2, keeping the scaling commensurate. The magnification affects all dimensions equally. When nrows != ncols we lose this perfect scaling, unavoidably, but we do the best we can by averaging the two dimensions.

factor = magnif * (double) (nrows+ncols) / 4.0

Here are the two main loops, the outermost passing down rows and the next passing across columns. Because we need neighbors of each pixel to compute the image, we cannot do the outer rows and columns.

```
row = 1
Begin row loop
   this_row = quat_dist + row * ncols          Current row in t matrix
   row_above = this_row - ncols
   row_below = this_row + ncols

   col = 1
   Begin column loop
      iptr = image + (row * ncols + col) * 3    24-bit RGB
```

Take care of three easy situations. If this ray missed the object, color this pixel pure black. Do the same if the three neighbors we will be examining all miss the object. Finally, for diagnostic purposes I give the user the ability to produce an image based strictly on the t values, the distances.

```
If this_row[col] <= MISS              This ray misses object?
   iptr[0] = iptr[1] = iptr[2] = 0
   Continue column loop, skipping subsequent computation

If ((row_above[col] <= MISS) && (row_below[col-1] <= MISS) &&
   (row_below[col+1] <= MISS))  All three neighbors miss?
   iptr[0] = iptr[1] = iptr[2] = 0
   Go to top of column loop, skipping subsequent computation

If lighting=0              No lighting (just distance-based tone)?
   iptr[0] = iptr[1] = iptr[2] = 127.0 + 30.0 * this_row[col]
   Continue column loop, skipping subsequent computation
```

In 3D display work it's easiest to work with triangles, because three points that are not collinear always define a plane. When processing a pixel, I arbitrarily choose to use the pixel directly above, that below/left, and that below/right. Get the 3D coordinates of these three points.

```
d = row_above[col] * factor
CosEl_d = CosEl * d
SinEl_d = SinEl * d
x1 = CosAz * (CosEl_d - SinEl)
y1 = SinAz * (CosEl_d - SinEl)
z1 = CosEl + SinEl_d
```

```
d = row_below[col-1] * factor
CosEl_d = CosEl * d
SinEl_d = SinEl * d
x2 = CosAz * (SinEl + CosEl_d) + SinAz
y2 = SinAz * (SinEl + CosEl_d) - CosAz
z2 = SinEl_d - CosEl

d = row_below[col+1] * factor
CosEl_d = CosEl * d
SinEl_d = SinEl * d
x3 = CosAz * (SinEl + CosEl_d) - SinAz
y3 = SinAz * (SinEl + CosEl_d) + CosAz
z3 = SinEl_d - CosEl
```

Now compute the surface normal of the triangle defined by these three pixels, and point it toward the eye.

```
x12d = x1 - x2
y12d = y1 - y2
z12d = z1 - z2
x23d = x2 - x3
y23d = y2 - y3
z23d = z2 - z3
x31d = x3 - x1
y31d = y3 - y1
z31d = z3 - z1
x12s = x1 + x2
y12s = y1 + y2
z12s = z1 + z2
x23s = x2 + x3
y23s = y2 + y3
z23s = z2 + z3
x31s = x3 + x1
y31s = y3 + y1
z31s = z3 + z1

xnor = y12d * z12s  +  y23d * z23s  +  y31d * z31s
ynor = z12d * x12s  +  z23d * x23s  +  z31d * x31s
znor = x12d * y12s  +  x23d * y23s  +  x31d * y31s

length = sqrt( 1.e-20 + xnor * xnor + ynor * ynor + znor * znor )
proj = xnor * xeye  +  ynor * yeye  +  znor * zeye
if (proj < 0.0)
   length = -length
```

```
    xnor /= length
    ynor /= length
    znor /= length
```

We're almost done. The last significant step is to compute the tone of this pixel according to the lighting and the surface normal.

```
If lighting = 1          Single white light at eye
   iptr[0] = iptr[1] = iptr[2] = 255.9 * proj / length

Else if lighting = 3       Single white light above
   proj = xnor * RlightX  +  ynor * RlightY  +  znor * RlightZ
   If proj > 0              Light must be on same side as eye!
     iptr[0] = iptr[1] = iptr[2] = 255.9 * proj
   else
     iptr[0] = iptr[1] = iptr[2] = 0    Black if light is on opposite side

Else if lighting = 2 || lighting = 4   3 RGB staggered; BGR order!
   proj = xnor * RlightX  +  ynor * RlightY  +  znor * RlightZ
   If proj > 0.0
     iptr[2] = 255.9 * proj
   Else
     iptr[2] = 0
   proj = xnor * GlightX  +  ynor * GlightY  +  znor * GlightZ
   If proj > 0.0
     iptr[1] = 255.9 * proj
   Else
     iptr[1] = 0
   proj = xnor * BlightX  +  ynor * BlightY  +  znor * BlightZ
   If proj > 0.0
     iptr[0] = 255.9 * proj
   Else
     iptr[0] = 0

 col = col + 1
 If col = ncols-1
    Break out of column loop
End column loop

row = row + 1
If row = nrows-1
   Break out of row loop

End row loop
```

I've left out a few minor steps in the algorithm that can be obtained from examining the C++ code in QUATERN.CPP. For example, the code just seen computes most of the image but omits the top and bottom rows and the leftmost and rightmost columns. This is because in order to get a triangle around the pixel being processed we need to go out one pixel in each direction. So the final step must be to fill in these missing rows and columns with the values just inside them.

Another item missing from this description is optional smoothing of the t values produced by **tracquat()**. This can sometimes slightly improve the appearance of the image. The smoothing code is trivial and not worth including in the text.

Finally, I apologize to readers who wish that I had included complete explanations of the 3D projection code just given. Unfortunately, such explanations would not only be well outside the scope of this text, but they are also widely available in many sources. My own personal recommendation for interested readers is *An Introduction to Ray Tracing* by Andrew Glassner. A more general reference is *Computer Graphics* by Steven Harrington. You'll find everything you need and more in these and similar books.

The JULIA Program

There are two mandatory and two optional steps involved in displaying a Mandelbrot or Julia image. These are:

1) From the *Parameters* menu select *Set parameters* and do so.
2) From the *File* menu select *Execute*. This computes and displays the image.
3) Optionally, from the *Parameters* menu select *Color map* to adjust the coloration of the displayed image. This is not valid for Quaternion displays.
4) Optionally, from the *Parameters* menu select *Magnify* to zoom in on a specific area of the image. This is not valid for Quaternion displays.

The Parameters Dialog

The user sets all required parameters in the *Parameters / Set parameters* dialog, which is shown in Figure 4.1 below, and a discussion follows.

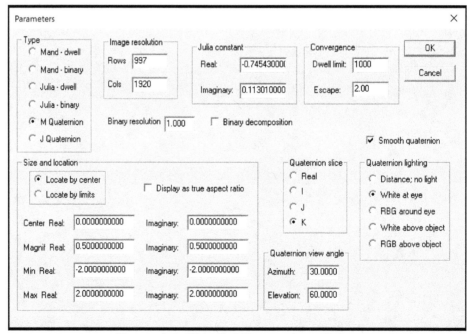

Figure 4.1: The *Set Parameters* dialog

Here is a brief summary of every parameter in this dialog box. More details are given later under individual topics.

Type - This specifies the nature of the object displayed, a standard Mandelbrot or Julia set, or a quaternion Mandelbrot or Julia set. For the standard (complex domain) set you can specify whether the definitional algorithm, which supplies dwells, is used, or the strictly binary but more detailed MSETDIST algorithm.

Image resolution - This is the number or rows and columns computed. It defaults to the resolution of the currently displayed main window. If the image will be saved to a file for printing it is recommended that the resolution be at least 300 pixels per printed inch. In this case it is also usually best to make the aspect ratio here equal the mathematical aspect ratio (real range divided by imaginary range), as this produces 'true' image scaling.

Binary resolution - This is used for only the binary (MSETDIST) versions of standard Mandelbrot and Julia sets. It controls the resolution for classifying pixels as members or nonmembers of the set, with smaller values producing more detail but also more ugly salt-and-pepper effect. This is the BinaryThreshold parameter in the code listing on Page 47. See the discussion a few pages before that listing for more details.

Binary Decomposition - This option is valid for only dwell-method Mandelbrot and Julia sets. If this box is checked, the low-order bit of the computed dwell is set according to the sign of the imaginary component of the last iterate. This was discussed on Page 39.

Julia constant - This is valid for only standard and quaternion Julia sets. It is the c parameter in the iteration. By default this starts out at a known 'pretty' value. If the user is displaying a Mandelbrot set and then uses the *Magnify* option, the Julia constant is reset to the coordinates of the center of the selected magnification rectangle.

Dwell limit - This is the maximum number of iterations that will be performed. It can have a great effect on computer time, but it should also be as large as is practical in most cases. It is especially important that it be large for the binary and quaternion versions of the object. It should also be large when at high magnification in high-dwell areas of the object. Certainly 1,000 would be a minimum requirement for most applications, and as large as 100,000 or more is not unreasonable in some cases.

Escape - This, the escape radius, is used for only the dwell version of the standard (complex domain) Mandelbrot and Julia sets. In most cases the default value of 2 is ideal, as it minimizes the amount of computer time required while still satisfying the member/nonmember decision rule. This is discussed in the section that begins on Page 40.

Many items appear in the *Size and location* block. There are two equivalent ways of specifying the size and location of the displayed block (for standard complex-domain versions) or the underlying block for the quaternion versions. We can either specify the minimum and maximum values of the real and imaginary components, or we can specify the real and imaginary centers and magnifications. Either of these methods completely specifies the other.

Center real/imaginary - This is the location of the center of the block

Magnif real/imaginary - This is the magnification in the horizontal and vertical directions.

Min real/imaginary - This is the minimum value of the real and imaginary coordinates of the displayed block. It corresponds to the lower/left corner of the block.

Max real/imaginary - This is the maximum value of the real and imaginary coordinates of the displayed block. It corresponds to the upper/right corner of the block.

Locate by center/limits - This determines which location method takes priority. If *Locate by center* is selected, when OK is pressed the min and max real and imaginary values will be updated to correspond to the specified values of the centers and magnifications. If *Locate by limits* is selected, when OK is pressed the centers and magnifications will be updated to correspond to the specified min and max real and imaginary parts. If displaying a quaternion object this defines the domain of the real and imaginary parts. This being the case, it is usually best to let them cover the full –2 to 2 range of the real and imaginary parts, although this is not required.

Display as true aspect ratio - This impacts the screen display and printing but has no effect on saved files, which always use the full specified resolution. If this box is not checked, the entire display window is filled with the image, regardless of the fact this will often distort the true aspect ratio. If this box is checked, the program assumes that the display pixels are square and fills the screen in accord with the true aspect ratio, resulting in a 'correct' displayed aspect ratio. This will usually result in the screen being only partially filled in one dimension.

All of the remaining parameters apply to quaternion displays only.

Quaternion slice - This specifies which of the four dimensions is sliced out.

Azimuth, Elevation - These determine the direction from which the eye views the object. If both are set to 0 we look at the object from infinitely far out on the +X axis. The Azimuth (0-360 degrees) is counterclockwise rotation around the Z (vertical) axis. The Elevation (0-90 degrees) is the angle that the view direction makes with the XY plane; an elevation of 90 degrees means that we are looking straight down at the object from infinitely far away in the +Z direction.

Smooth quaternion - If checked this applies a very mild smoothing to the quaternion object. The effect is subtle but usually good. The reason is that often the object will have an extremely rough surface that causes an unpleasant salt-and-pepper effect as adjacent surfaces alternate reflecting and not reflecting light. Smoothing greatly lessens this effect.

Quaternion lighting - This specifies the way the object is illuminated. The choices are:

Distance, no light - This choice is for diagnostic purposes only. Rather than lighting the object, the displayed tone of each pixel is determined by the distance of the object from the eye.

White at eye - This places a single white light coming from the direction of the eye. In most cases this is the best choice; it's like reading a book with a light behind your head; everything that the eye can see is illuminated from a uniform direction.

RGB around eye - This places three pure colored lights (red, green, blue) in a circle around the eye. The effect is somewhat similar to having a single white light at the eye, but since none of the lights is exactly in line with the eye, and each hits the object from a slightly different direction, the object is colored in ways that are sometimes beautiful and sometimes just confusing.

White above object - A single white light is placed infinitely far out on the +Z axis. This is most effective when the elevation is large (like the light, the eye is looking down from on high).

RGB above object - Red, green, and blue lights are shining down on the object from the +Z axis, but they are not collinear. Rather, they are staggered equally so that they impact the object from slightly different directions. Sometimes this is great, but often it's just confusing.

The Colormap Dialog

For standard (complex-domain) Mandelbrot or Julia sets the user can control how dwells or binary classifications map to displayed colors. The colormap option is not applicable to Quaternion displays. When the user selects *Parameters / Colormap*, the dialog shown in Figure 4.2 appears.

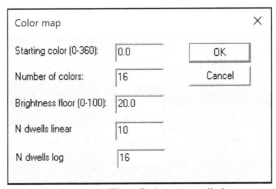

Figure 4.2 The Colormap dialog

If the dwell version of computation was used, the dwells will have a maximum value of the user-specified Dwell Limit. For the binary (MSETDIST) version the 'dwells' will be zero for nonmembers of the set and one for members.

The colormap behaves somewhat differently according to whether the *Number of colors* is zero or nonzero.

If *Number of colors* is zero, the image is strictly binary, a single shade of gray versus pure white, alternating according to several rules. The gray level is specified by the *Brightness floor*, with 0 being pure black. Tones strictly alternate for increasing dwells until the dwell reaches *N dwells linear*. After that point the tones alternate according to the log of the dwell, with the range divided into *N dwells log* bins that are equally spaced in the log domain. Using larger values of these two quantities results in finer detail being displayed, at the expense of a more cluttered, salt-and-pepper appearance. The program does make sure that the tone at Dwell Limit is the opposite of the tone at Dwell Limit minus one.

Considerable experimentation is usually required to provide a good display, although with a little practice the effect of these quantities will become well understood.

The *Starting color* lets the user reverse the tone assignment. If it is set to zero there will be one assignment, and if it is set to any nonzero value the result will be the negative of the tone assignment.

If *Number of colors* is positive (negatives are not allowed) then the image is colored (hue) using the specified number of colors, and the brightness is a monotonic function of the dwell.

Each dwell that is less than or equal to *N dwells linear* is assigned to its own unique bin. Dwells greater than this are divided into *N dwells log* bins that are equally space in the log domain. Because a dwell of zero is possible, there are a total of *N dwells linear* + *N dwells log* + 1 bins that are in a monotonic relationship with the dwell.

Colors (hue) are assigned to the bins in rotation with a period of *Number of colors* and beginning with *Starting color*, which is specified in degrees (0-360) around the standard color pallette. See any good textbook on color for details. Tone is assigned monotonically with the bin, starting with *Brightness floor*. This is a percent (0-100) of full white. To make the brightness independent of dwell, using full brightness for all dwells, specify 100 for the *Brightness floor*.

The Magnify Dialog

If a standard (complex domain) Mandelbrot or Julia set is displayed, the user can select an area of it for magnification. This is done by clicking the *Parameters / Magnify* menu option. A movable display will appear showing the size/location parameters of the current rectangle, which is also displayed whenever a mouse button is pressed. Move the entire rectangle by pressing the left mouse button, and move the lower-right corner (thus controlling the size) by pressing the right mouse button. A degree of movement magnification is employed, meaning that the rectangle moves less than the mouse, which enables more precise adjustment.

If a Mandelbrot set is being displayed, the Julia parameters in the main parameter menu will be changed to the location of the center of the displayed rectangle when OK is clicked.

Displaying a Julia Set

As stated just above, when a Mandelbrot set is displayed and the *Magnify* option is employed, the Julia parameters are set to the location of the center of the magnification rectangle. Moreover, if a Julia object type is selected immediately after a Mandelbrot set, the size/location parameters will be changed to encompass the entire –2 to 2 domain of the real and imaginary components. This enables initial display of the entire Julia set.

Note that this magnification method is a great way of selecting the region of the Mandelbrot set that defines the desired Julia set. The usual procedure would be to shrink the magnification rectangle to its minimum size and then precisely locate its center to define the Julia set.

Examples

This section contains some assorted examples of using the *JULIA* program. Figure 4.5 on the next page shows the Julia set defined by the real and imaginary Julia parameters that are the default when the program starts. This image employed the dwell algorithm. Figure 4.6 is the same Julia set, but computed using the binary MSETDIST algorithm. The resemblance should be obvious, but notice how each method reveals its own type of information and has its own beauty. Finally, in Figures 4.3 and 4.4 below we see two different views of the quaternion version of this same Julia set.

Figure 4.3: Quaternion Julia set

Figure 4.4: Quaternion Julia set

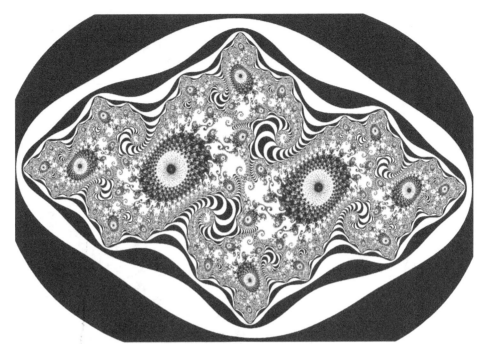

Figure 4.5: A Julia set computed by the dwell method

Figure 4.6: The same Julia set computed by the MSETDIST method

Figure 4.7 below shows the complete Mandelbrot set as computed with the binary MSETDIST method. The magnification box and associated size/location parameter box are also shown.

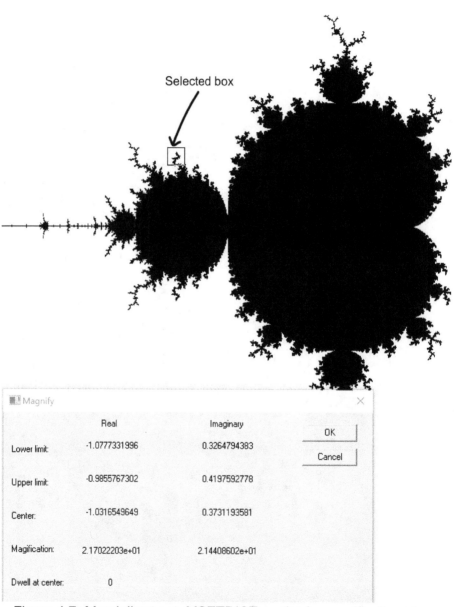

Figure 4.7: Mandelbrot set, MSETDIST method, magnification shown

Figure 4.8 below shows the contents of the magnification block of the prior figure. A new magnification block is also shown.

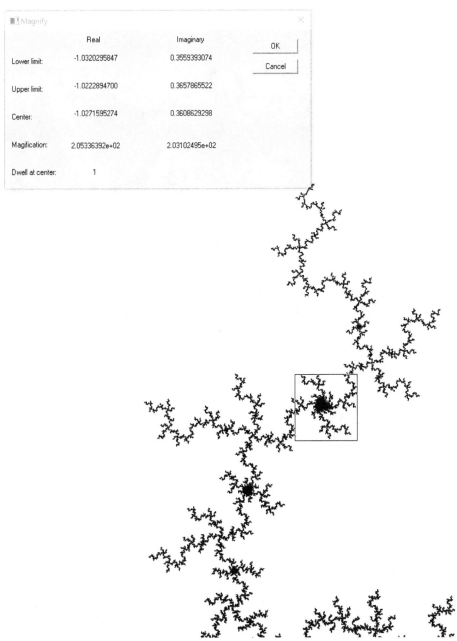

Figure 4.8: Exploded view from the prior figure

Figure 4.9 below is the magnification block from the prior figure. We now switch from the binary method to the dwell method. Note the appearance of a tiny Mandelbrot set, which I surrounded with a magnification block. Being limited to black-and-white is a serious artistic limitation. In full color, images like this are magnificent.

Figure 4.9: Exploded view from the prior figure, dwell method

Figure 4.10 below is the final image in this sequence, although the Julia program can go much, much further. Again, this tiny region within the Mandelbrot set was computed with the dwell method. No matter how deep you go, new Mandelbrot shapes keep appearing. The main problem that limits practical display depth is that dwells increase rapidly at high magnification of interesting places. Figure 4.10 used a Dwell Limit of 10,000, and that would have to jump to at least 100,000 at the next magnification level. Run times can become prohibitive, usually before floating-point issues impose their own limitations.

Figure 4.10: A Mandelbrot shape deep inside the complete set

I'll end this presentation with a quick Julia set demonstration. You already saw some Julia sets in Figures 4.3 through 4.6 beginning on Page 73. For this demonstration I began with the Mandelbrot set and a tiny magnification rectangle, shown in Figure 4.11 below. This operation causes the Julia parameters to be reset to the center of the rectangle.

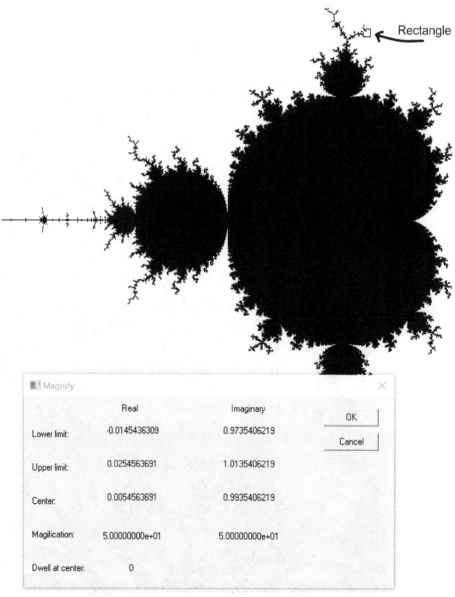

Figure 4.11: Finding a location for a Julia set

Now I switched to a Julia set with the binary (MSETDIST) method. Switching from Mandelbrot to Julia causes the displayed range to expand to the full −2 to 2 in both the real and imaginary dimensions. This fairly uninteresting image is shown in Figure 4.12 below.

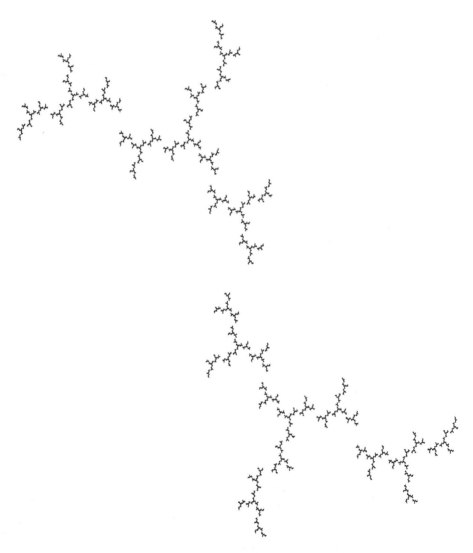

Figure 4.12: Julia set defined by center of prior figure's rectangle

But this set becomes a lot more interesting when computed and viewed in the quaternion domain. Two views are shown in Figures 4.13 and 4.14.

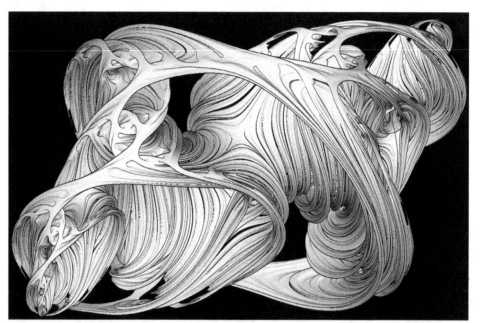

Figure 4.13: Quaternion version of prior Julia set

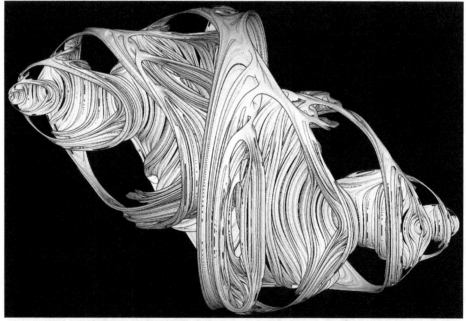

Figure 4.14: Same set from a different view angle

Lindenmayer Systems

Aristid Lindenmayer was a Hungarian biologist who, in 1968, developed numerous mathematical systems for modeling the growth of plants and some other living organisms. To a considerable but not universal degree these involved fractal properites, meaning (roughly) that the same patterns appear repeatedly at smaller and smaller scales. Other Lindenmayer systems (*L-systems*) and their relatives involved iterations of surprisingly simple equations. This chapter will present several of Lindenmayer's more accessible systems, as well as close relatives. Much of this material is from the classic book by Przemyslaw Prusinkiewicz and Aristid Lindenmayer (1990), *The Algorithmic Beauty of Plants*.

Edge Rewriting

One of the simplest L-systems is *edge rewriting*. Despite its simplicity, edge rewriting is capable of producing many interesting and artistic patterns, and can be ideal for producing decorative borders or panel fills.

In order to describe a shape, though in an admittedly limited yet effective way, we need a language. The language generally used with edge rewriting is often called a *turtle* interpretation, in analogy with a turtle lumbering along a path. The most basic turtle language defines a fixed angle for turns and a fixed distance for moves. The angle is measured counterclockwise from the +X axis (pointing to the right as the object is seen). A 'sentence' in this turtle language basically says things like "Take three steps, turn right, take one step, turn right again, take a step, turn left, take a step...". In particular, this most basic form requires only three symbols:

P Take a step, drawing a line as we go
+ Turn left (increase the counterclockwise angle)
− Turn right (decrease the angle)

By convention the turtle starts its journey pointing to the right, the +X direction. Using an angle of 90 degrees, Figure 5.2 on the next page illustrates the path mentioned in the prior paragraph. This path is described by the string PPP-P-P+P.

The simplest edge rewriting system is defined by the fixed angle and two entities: The *axiom* is a starting shape, which may be as trivial as a single line, or may describe a complex shape. The *production* is the rule that shows how each step (P) is to be replaced with a more complex string. We also need to specify how many times this replacement will be performed.

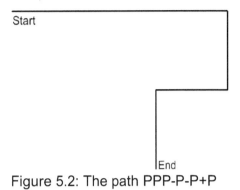

Figure 5.2: The path PPP-P-P+P

For example, consider the *quadratic Koch island*, which is defined using a 90 degree angle and the following axiom and production. Figure 5.3 on the next page depicts the axiom, and the subsequent figures show successive edge replacement iterations.

Axiom: P–P–P–P
Production: P–P+P+PP–P–P+P

We get the first iteration string by replacing every P in the axiom with the entire production. This is shown below. Subsequent iteration strings become too long and unwieldy to show written out. Just imagine if we replaced every P in this string with the entire production!

P–P+P+PP–P–P+P–P–P+P+PP–P–P+P–P–P+P+PP–P–P+P–P–P+P+PP–P–P+P

It should be clear now how the term *edge replacement* describes this system. Each step (P) produces an edge, with the stipulation that multiple contiguous steps are interpreted as multiple edges, even though visually they may appear as a single longer edge. When we replace each P in a string with the production, we are replacing that edge with a more complex string. The resulting figure is fractal because shape details remain the same at multiple scales.

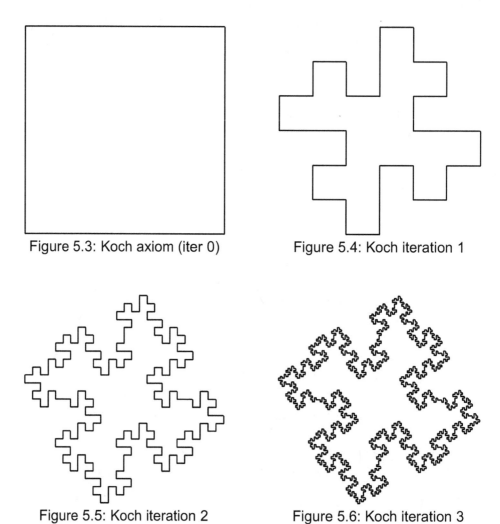

Figure 5.3: Koch axiom (iter 0)   Figure 5.4: Koch iteration 1

Figure 5.5: Koch iteration 2   Figure 5.6: Koch iteration 3

Multiple Productions

We need not be limited to a single production; any number may be used. However, two productions are sufficient for a vast array of possible shapes, so the *LIN* program is limited to two here. When there are multiple productions, we use the same number of different symbols for a step. Each such symbol is still interpreted as a single step (edge); in terms of the turtle interpretation there is no difference between them. However, the identity of a step determines which production replaces it.

I used the letter P to represent a step because P is the first letter of *Primary*. This lets us use S for a secondary production.

One of the most famous L-system patterns is the *Sierpinski gasket*, shown after seven iterations in Figure 5.7. This pattern requires an angle of 60 degrees and two productions:

Axiom: S
Primary production: S+P+S
Secondary production: P–S–P

Don't be confused by the use of two different symbols (P and S) to represent edges. They are identical in terms of movement, a single step in the current direction. The symbol just tells us which production to use when the edge is replaced.

Figure 5.7: Sierpinski gasket iteration 7

Examples of Edge Replacement

This lovely 'lace doily'
is produced from 4
iterations of:
Axiom: P–P–P–P
Prod: PP–P–P–P–P–P+P
with angle=90 degrees.

You can make it a tad
less busy by using just 3
iterations.

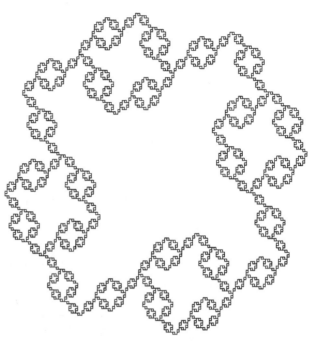

A trivial change to
the production
dramatically changes
the pattern.

Axiom: P–P–P–P
Prod: PP–P–P–P–P–P+P
with angle=90 degrees.

This intricate decorative pattern is obtained from 4 iterations of

Axiom: P–P–P–P
Prod: PP–P–P–P–PP
Angle=90 degrees

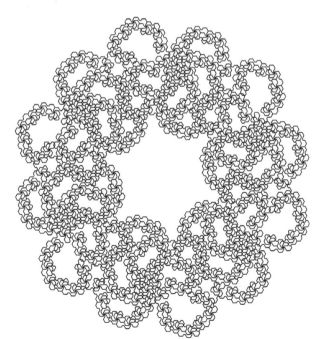

We can head in the direction of snowflakes by going with an angle of 60 degrees and 6 moves in the axiom.

Axiom: P-P-P-P-P-P
Prod: P-PP-PP-PP+P

Edge Replacement in LIN

If you select "Edge Replacement" from the Image menu, the following dialog box appears:

```
┌─────────────────────────────────────────────────────────────┐
│ Edge rewriting parameters                                 ✕  │
│                                                              │
│         Rows: │500        │      ┌──────────────────┐        │
│                                  │        OK        │        │
│                                  └──────────────────┘        │
│         Cols: │500        │                                  │
│                                         Cancel               │
│   Line width │3           │                                  │
│                                                              │
│                                                              │
│        Depth │1          │       Angle │90.00      │         │
│                                                              │
│       Axiom  │                                    │          │
│                                                              │
│     Primary  │                                    │          │
│                                                              │
│   Secondary  │                                    │          │
│                                                              │
└─────────────────────────────────────────────────────────────┘
```

Rows - The row resolution of the image. It is strongly recommended that this equal the column resolution to avoid distortions.

Cols - The column resolution of the image. It is strongly recommended that this equal the row resolution to avoid distortions.

Line width - This is the thickness (in pixels) of the lines drawn. It should be odd; if an even number is specified, it is incremented.

Depth - The number of iterations, with 0 meaning that only the axiom is plotted. If nonzero, a primary production must be specified.

Angle - The fixed angle, which must be from 0 through 90 degrees.

Axiom - The axiom, which must always be supplied. Case (upper/lower) is ignored. Spaces may be included for clarity and are ignored. The only legal characters are P, S, +, and -.

Primary - The primary production, which must be supplied if the Depth in nonzero. Spaces may be included for clarity and are ignored. The only legal characters are P, S, +, and -.

Secondary - The secondary production, which must be supplied if either the axiom or the primary production contain the letter S. Spaces may be included for clarity and are ignored. The only legal characters are P, S, +, and -.

The generated image will be in correct scale if the row and column resolution are equal. It will be expanded in such a way that the image almost touches both the left and bottom edges of the display area, and in addition either the top of the image almost touches the top of the display area, or the right edge of the image almost touches the right side of the display area (or both).

Algorithms and code

In this section I'll present an assortment of algorithms that implement edge-replacement L-systems. Complete C++ code is in the file COMPUTE_ER.CPP. For clarity, here I'll omit memory allocation, error checking, and other mundane details.

The overall program flow includes three steps. First we iteratively expand the operation string, beginning with the axiom and performing as many edge replacement iterations as the user requests (the *Depth*). Second, we convert the final operation string into turtle move coordinates, scaled to a square with horizontal and vertical dimensions in the range 0-1. Third and lastly, we generate a binary image of the user-specified resolution based on the movements of the turtle. This can be shown as follows:

```
Successor = Axiom
Repeat Depth times
   Predecessor = Successor
   Successor = Expand ( Predecessor )
TurtleMoves = Turtle ( Successor )
Image = MakeImage ( TurtleMoves )
```

The expand-by-replacement routine is straightforward. It is given the following quantities:

n	Number of tokens in source
source[]	Source string (predecessor)
dest[]	Destination string (successor)
n_primary	Number of primary production tokens (positive)
primary[]	They are here
n_secondary[]	Number of secondary production tokens (may be zero)
secondary[]	They are here

All this routine does is replace the P and S moves with their corresponding productions, and copy everything else. It returns to the caller the number of tokens in the successor string. The algorithm is shown on the next page.

```
j = 0                        This will count and index successor terms
For i from 0 through n-1     Pass through entire predecessor string

   If source[i] = '+'        Just copy
      dest[j] = '+'
      j = j + 1

   If source[i] = '-'        Just copy
      dest[j] = '-'
      j = j + 1

   If source[i] = 'P'        Primary production
      For k from 0 through n_primary-1
         dest[j] = primary[k]
         j = j + 1

   If source[i] = 'S'        Secondary production
      For k from 0 through n_secondary-1
         dest[j] = secondary[k]
         j = j + 1

Return j                     The number of tokens in successor
```

The **Turtle** routine is somewhat longer, although each individual component is simple. It is given the following quantities:

```
n          Number of operations in 'opstr'
opstr[]    The operation string
angle      Angle (0-90 degrees) by which to turn; + means CCW
x[]        Output of x coordinates of nodes
y[]        And y coordinates
```

The turtle starts at coordinates (0, 0) and with angle=0, meaning that it is pointing to the right (out the +X axis). We let it travel unimpeded but keep track of its range so that after its journey is complete we can scale it to being slightly inside a unit square.

One part of this algorithm that might be confusing is that we regularly 'touch up' its jumps and angle changes. Its position and direction are cumulated along its journey. Especially if there are an enormous number of moves, which is not uncommon, tiny floating-point errors may build up to the extent that the turtle fails to connect with a point that it should theoretically align with. We may end up with line segments that are supposed to connect but that actually miss by one pixel. In order to minimize the possibility of this happening we adjust moves and angles to be exact whenever possible. Because exact vertical and horizontal lines are common in edge replacement, such fixes are generally easy and effective.

```
angle = angle * PI / 180.0                    Convert degrees to radians
current_x = current_y = current_angle = 0.0
xmin = xmax = ymin = ymax = 0.0               Boundary of the figure

x[0] = y[0] = 0.0                             Path starts here
node = 1                                      Index into x and y arrays

For i from 0 through n–1

   If opstr[i] = '+'                          Turn CCW
      current_angle = current_angle + angle
      If current_angle >= 2 * PI             Keep angle in 0-360 degrees
        current_angle = current_angle – 2 * PI

   Else If opstr[i] = '–'                     Turn CW
      current_angle = current_angle – angle
      If current_angle < 0                   Keep angle in 0-360 degrees
        current_angle = current_angle + 2 * PI

   Else If opstr[i] = 'P'  OR  opstr[i] = 'S'    Take a step

      Periodically reset angle to exact value to prevent error cumulation
      If AbsVal ( current_angle ) < tiny
        current_angle = 0
      Else If AbsVal ( current_angle – PI / 2 ) < tiny
        current_angle = PI / 2
      Else If AbsVal ( current_angle – PI) < tiny
        current_angle = PI
      Else If AbsVal ( current_angle – 3 * PI / 2 ) < tiny
        current_angle = 3 * PI / 2

      cos_a = cos ( current_angle )
      sin_a = sin ( current_angle )
```

Make sure vertical/horizontal moves are perfect
If AbsVal (cos_a) < tiny
   cos_a = 0
Else If AbsVal (cos_a − 1) < tiny
   cos_a = 1
Else If AbsVal (cos_a + 1) < tiny
   cos_a = −1
If AbsVal (sin_a) < tiny
   sin_a = 0
Else If AbsVal (sin_a − 1.0) < tiny
   sin_a = 1
Else If AbsVal (sin_a + 1) < tiny
   sin_a = −1

current_x += cos_a
current_y += sin_a

If current_x < xmin
   xmin = current_x
If current_x > xmax
   xmax = current_x
If current_y < ymin
   ymin = current_y
If current_y > ymax
   ymax = current_y

x[node] = current_x
y[node] = current_y
node = node + 1

The nodes are computed. Shift and scale so the figure almost touches the bottom and left sides, as well as either the top or right side or both.

If xmax − xmin > ymax − ymin
   scale = 0.98 / (xmax − xmin)
Else
   scale = 0.98 / (ymax - ymin)

For i from 0 through node−1
   x[i] = scale * (x[i] - xmin) + 0.01
   y[i] = scale * (y[i] - ymin) + 0.01

return node   *Tell the caller how many nodes we have*

The MakeImage routine that draws lines in an nrows by ncols raster image to connect turtle nodes is too complex to reproduce in detail here, so I'll just present an outline. The DrawLine routine referenced below is the standard Bresenham algorithm, widely available from many sources. Here is the outline:

Initialize image to all white

xa = Round (ncols * x[0])
ya = Round (nrows * y[0])

For node from 1 through Nnodes–1
    xb = Round (ncols * x[node])
    yb = Round (nrows * y[node])

    DrawLine from (xa, ya) through (xb, yx)

    xa = xb
    ya = yb

If you examine this build_image() routine in COMPUTE_ER.CPP you will see that I use an approach to line width that is shockingly inefficient but that is still so fast that ineffiency does not matter. The 'standard' way to draw lines whose width is greater than one is to run two Bresenham algorithms in parallel, thereby creating upper/lower or left/right bounds, and fill in the pixels between the bounds. However, this requires complex corrections when lines join at oblique angles. The much simpler approach is to run a single Bresenham algorithm and draw circles of appropriate radius along its extent. Naturally, this results in a vast number of pixels that are needlessly set to black multiple times, when just once is enough! However, this method automatically creates smooth turning points and hence is my choice in this application that already runs extremely quickly.

Axial Generation

The prior section described *edge rewriting*. Another L-system that is nearly as simple is often called *axial generation*. Like the former, it employs a mandatory axiom and at least one production. At most two productions are allowed in the *LIN* program. However, rather than recursively replacing edges with new, more complex sets of edges, axial generation recursively replaces edges with *axial trees*. This is not the forum for a detailed graph-theoretic definition of this term; you can find definitions easily online and in more mathematically oriented books. For our purposes, we consider a tree to be a collection of line segments that begin at a *root node* and branch upward and outward to *terminal nodes*. A characteristic of an axial tree is that at each of its nodes there is at most one segment going straight ahead; all other branches go off at an angle.

Axial generation, like edge replacement, has a simple *turtle* interpretation. It similarly defines a fixed angle for turns and a fixed distance for moves. Axial generation also shares three symbols with edge replacement:

P Take a step, drawing a line as we go
+ Turn left (increase the counterclockwise angle)
– Turn right (decrease the angle)

However, axial generation requires two additional symbols in order to facilitate multiple branches from the same node:

[Push the current status onto a stack to preserve it
] Pop the saved status off the top of the stack and restore this status

I also include one additional symbol that is not required but that helps with realism:

V Decrease line width by a fixed multiplier

By convention the axial generation turtle starts its journey pointing directly upward, the +Y direction.

Those bracket symbols that push and pop turtle status onto and from the stack need some discussion for the sake of non-programmers. Perhaps you have seen stacks of dishes in buffet restaurants (which no longer exist as I write this in the midst of a global pandemic!). There is a big pile of clean dishes. When the dishwasher has a newly washed dish ready for customers, he places it on the top of the stack rather than trying to squeeze it into the middle somewhere. And when a customer wants a clean dish, he takes it from the top of the stack, rather than trying to slip it out from the middle. Turtle stacks operate the same way.

The turtle has a status at all times. At a minimum the status will include the x and y coordinates of the current position, as well as the angle in which it is pointing. In our case there is one more status item, the current thickness of the line being drawn. When a left bracket ([) is encountered, these status items are saved (pushed) onto the top of a stack. When the right bracket (]) is encountered, the current status is replaced by the status most recently pushed onto the stack, an action called *popping* the stack.

Consider the following simple system:
Axiom: P
Production: P[+P][-P]P

The axiom P is just a single vertical line. Replacing P once (iteration 1) with the production says to move straight ahead (recall we start pointing up) one unit and then save our status. Turn left by the fixed angle, take one step, and then restore our status. Save our status again, turn right, take one step, and restore our status. Finally take one step. This gives us Figure 5.13 below. The status being saved and restored is the central intersection.

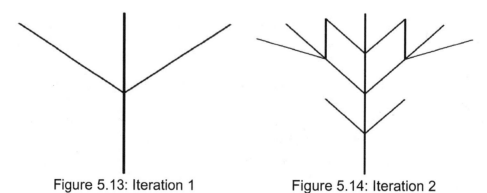

Figure 5.13: Iteration 1   Figure 5.14: Iteration 2

One more replacement iteration gives the following operation string:

P[+P][-P]P[+P[+P][-P]P][-P[+P][-P]P]P[+P][-P]P

I'll leave it as an exercise for the reader to verify the substitutions that occurred and to confirm that this operation string produces Figure 5.14.

The utility of being able to shrink lines is made apparent in Figure 5.15 below. This was generated with 6 iterations, an angle of 25 degrees, and a shrink factor of 0.8. The axiom and productions are:
Axiom: S
Primary: PP
Secondary: P[VV+S]P[VV-S]+VS

Let's trace the path of the first iteration. Take a step (straight up) and save the status. Shrink twice, turn left, take a step, and restore the status (position, angle, and line width). Step up and save the status. Shrink twice, turn right, take a step, and restore the status. Turn left, shrink once, and take a step. If we did not shrink smaller branches, the image would not only be unnatural, but would also be overlapped and blurred.

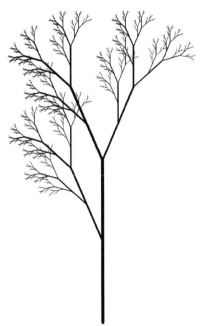

Figure 5.15: Shrinking lines

Stem Length Between Branches

Figure 5.16: No primary production

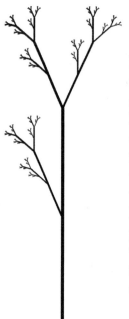

Look back at Figure 5.15 and the pair of productions that created it. The role of the secondary production should be clear; it generates the branching pattern. But the primary production PP might not be initially clear. Think about its effect as we iterate. P is the forward motion, spacing between branches. Using the PP production, this forward distance doubles with every iteration, placing more space between lateral branches. Figure 5.16 changes the primary production to just P, meaning that no increase occurs, while Figure 5.17 uses PPP to triple the forward motion between branches. These two figures should make the effect of the primary production clear.

Figure 5.17: PPP

Axial Generation in LIN

If you select "Axial generation" from the Image menu, the following dialog box appears:

```
┌─────────────────────────────────────────────────────────────┐
│ Axial growth parameters                                    × │
│                                                              │
│        Rows:  500              ┌──────────────┐              │
│                                │      OK      │              │
│                                └──────────────┘              │
│         Cols:  500                  Cancel                   │
│                                                              │
│   Line width  3         Line shrink factor  1.00             │
│                                                              │
│        Depth  1                     Angle  90.00             │
│                                                              │
│       Axiom  ┌──────────────────────────────────┐           │
│                                                              │
│     Primary  ┌──────────────────────────────────┐           │
│                                                              │
│   Secondary  ┌──────────────────────────────────┐           │
│                                                              │
└─────────────────────────────────────────────────────────────┘
```

Rows - The row resolution of the image. It is strongly recommended that this equal the column resolution to avoid distortions.

Cols - The column resolution of the image. It is strongly recommended that this equal the row resolution to avoid distortions.

Line width - This is the thickness (in pixels) of the *thickest* lines drawn. It should be odd; if an even number is specified, it is incremented.

Depth - The number of iterations, with 0 meaning that only the axiom is plotted. If nonzero, a primary production must be specified.

Angle - The fixed angle, which must be from 0 through 90 degrees.

Axiom - The axiom, which must always be supplied. Case (upper/lower) is ignored. Spaces may be included for clarity and are ignored. The only legal characters are P, S, V, [,], +, and -.

Primary - The primary production, which must be supplied if the Depth in nonzero. Spaces may be included for clarity and are ignored. The only legal characters are P, S, V, [,], +, and -.

Secondary - The secondary production, which must be supplied if either the axiom or the primary production contain the letter S. Spaces may be included for clarity and are ignored. The only legal characters are P, S, V, [,], +, and -.

Line shrink factor - Every time **V** is encountered in an operation string the thickness of subsequent lines drawn will be reduced by multiplication by this factor, which should not exceed 1. The current line thickness is saved on the stack and restored along with the position and direction.

The generated image will be in correct scale if the row and column resolution are equal. It will be expanded in such a way that the image almost touches both the left and bottom edges of the display area, and in addition either the top of the image almost touches the top of the display area, or the right edge of the image almost touches the right side of the display area (or both).

Algorithms and Code

In this section I'll present an assortment of algorithms that implement axial-generation L-systems. Complete C++ code is in the file COMPUTE_AG.CPP. For clarity, here I'll omit memory allocation, error checking, and other mundane details.

The overall program flow includes the same three steps as edge replacement. First we iteratively expand the operation string, beginning with the axiom and performing as many iterations as the user requests (the *Depth*). Second, we convert the final operation string into turtle move coordinates, scaled to a square with horizontal and vertical dimensions in the range 0-1. Third and lastly, we generate a binary image of the user-specified resolution based on the movements of the turtle. This can be shown as follows:

```
Successor = Axiom
Repeat Depth times
   Predecessor = Successor
   Successor = Expand ( Predecessor )
TurtleMoves = Turtle ( Successor )
Image = MakeImage ( TurtleMoves )
```

The expand-by-replacement routine (called advance() in the C++ code) is straightforward. It is given the following quantities:

n	Number of tokens in source
source[]	Source string (predecessor)
dest[]	Destination string (successor)
n_primary	Number of primary production tokens (positive)
primary[]	They are here
n_secondary[]	Number of secondary production tokens (may be zero)
secondary[]	They are here

All this routine does is replace the P and S moves with their corresponding productions, and copy everything else. It returns to the caller the number of tokens in the successor string. The algorithm is shown on the next page.

```
j = 0                        This will count and index successor terms
For i from 0 through n–1     Pass through entire predecessor string

  If source[i] = '+'         Just copy
    dest[j] = '+'
    j = j + 1

  If source[i] = '-'         Just copy
    dest[j] = '-'
    j = j + 1

  If source[i] = '['         Just copy
    dest[j] = '['
    j = j + 1

  If source[i] = ']'         Just copy
    dest[j] = ']'
    j = j + 1

  If source[i] = 'V'         Just copy
    dest[j] = 'V'
    j = j + 1

  If source[i] = 'P'         Primary production
    For k from 0 through n_primary–1
      dest[j] = primary[k]
      j = j + 1

  If source[i] = 'S'         Secondary production
    For k from 0 through n_secondary–1
      dest[j] = secondary[k]
      j = j + 1

Return j                     The number of tokens in successor
```

The axial-generation Turtle routine is somewhat longer and more complex than that for edge replacement, although each individual component is simple. It is given the following quantities:

n	Number of operations in 'opstr'
opstr[]	The operation string
angle	Angle (0-90 degrees) by which to turn; + means CCW
shrink	Line width shrink factor
width	Initial (thickest) line width
x[]	Output of x coordinates of nodes
y[]	And y coordinates
thickness[]	Output of line thickness
draw_line[]	Flags whether a move is to also draw a line
stack_x	Work area
stack_y	Work area
stack_a	Work area
stack_t	Work area

The turtle starts at coordinates (0, 0) and with angle=90 degrees, meaning that it is pointing straight up (out the +Y axis). We let it travel unimpeded but keep track of its range so that after its journey is complete we can scale it to being slightly inside a unit square.

```
angle = angle * PI / 180.0            Convert degrees to radians
current_x = current_y = 0.0
current_angle = PI / 2
current_thickness = width
xmin = xmax = ymin = ymax = 0.0       Boundary of the figure

x[0] = y[0] = 0.0                     Path starts here
node = 1                              Index into x and y arrays
```

For i from 0 through n–1

```
   If opstr[i] = '+'                          Turn CCW
      current_angle = current_angle + angle
      If current_angle >= 2 * PI             Keep angle in 0-360 degrees
         current_angle = current_angle – 2 * PI

   Else If opstr[i] = '–'                     Turn CW
      current_angle = current_angle – angle
      If current_angle < 0                   Keep angle in 0-360 degrees
         current_angle = current_angle + 2 * PI
```

```
Else If opstr[i] = 'V'                    Shrink line thickness
   current_thickness = current_thickness * shrink
   If current_thickness < 1.0
      current_thickness = 1.0

Else If opstr[i] = 'P'  OR  opstr[i] = 'S'    Take a step
   cos_a = cos ( current_angle )
   sin_a = sin ( current_angle )

   current_x += cos_a
   current_y += sin_a

   If current_x < xmin
      xmin = current_x
   If current_x > xmax
      xmax = current_x
   If current_y < ymin
      ymin = current_y
   If  current_y > ymax
      ymax = current_y

   x[node] = current_x
   y[node] = current_y
   thickness[node] = current_thickness
   draw_line[node] = True
   node = node + 1

Else If opstr[i] = '['                    Push state onto stack
   stack_x[kstack] = current_x
   stack_y[kstack] = current_y
   stack_a[kstack] = current_angle
   stack_t[kstack] = current_thickness
   kstack = kstack + 1

Else If opstr[i] = ']'                    Pop state from stack
   kstack = kstack - 1
   current_x = stack_x[kstack]
   current_y = stack_y[kstack]
   current_angle = stack_a[kstack]
   current_thickness = stack_t[kstack]
   x[node] = current_x
   y[node] = current_y
   // No need to get thickness because no line drawn; just moved
   draw_line[node] = False
   node = node + 1
```

The nodes are computed. Shift and scale so the figure almost touches the bottom and left sides, as well as either the top or right side or both.

If xmax – xmin > ymax – ymin
  scale = 0.98 / (xmax – xmin)
Else
  scale = 0.98 / (ymax - ymin)

For i from 0 through node–1
  x[i] = scale * (x[i] - xmin) + 0.01
  y[i] = scale * (y[i] - ymin) + 0.01

return node   *Tell the caller how many nodes we have*

The MakeImage routine that draws lines in an nrows by ncols raster image to connect turtle nodes is too complex to reproduce in detail here, so I'll just present an outline. The DrawLine routine referenced below is the standard Bresenham algorithm, widely available from many sources. Here is the outline:

Initialize image to all white

xa = Round (ncols * x[0])
ya = Round (nrows * y[0])

For node from 1 through Nnodes–1
  xb = Round (ncols * x[node])
  yb = Round (nrows * y[node])

  If (NOT draw_line[node])
    xa = xb ;
    ya = yb ;
    Go to top of node loop, skipping remaining loop code

  DrawLine from (xa, ya) through (xb, yx)

  xa = xb
  ya = yb

If you examine this build_image() routine in COMPUTE_AG.CPP you will see that I use an approach to line width that is shockingly inefficient but that is still so fast that inefficiency does not matter. The 'standard' way to draw lines whose width is greater than one is to run two Bresenham algorithms in parallel, thereby creating upper/lower or left/right bounds, and fill in the pixels between the bounds. However, this requires complex corrections when lines join at oblique angles. The much simpler approach is to run a single Bresenham algorithm and draw circles of appropriate radius along its extent. Naturally, this results in a vast number of pixels that are needlessly set to black multiple times, when just once is enough! However, this method automatically creates smooth turning points and hence is my choice in this application that already runs extremely quickly.

Axial Generation in Three Dimensions

The technique of the prior section can be generalized to three dimensions, in which case the turtle's path is a 'line' having diameter (really a cylinder) rather than a 'line' having width (really a rectangle). Not surprisingly, this requires some additional notation, and it is also helpful to slightly change some existing notation. The complete set of commands is shown below, and they will be described in detail in subsequent sections.

F Take a step forward. This was performed by *P* and *S* in the two prior sections.

+ Turn left. In aeronautics this is called *yaw*.

– Turn right.

^ Pitch up, as in an airplane taking off.

& Pitch down, as in an airplane diving toward the ground.

**** Roll left, as in an airplane dipping its left wing down and right wing up.

/ Roll right.

| Turn around (reverse direction)

V Shrink the diameter of the cylinder being drawn.

[Push the current turtle state onto a stack.

] Pop the stack to restore the turtle state.

C# Set the color to one of ten choices, where # is a digit from 0 through 9.

{ Start definition of a filled polygon, and push state onto stack.

} End definition of filled polygon and pop state from stack.

S Take a step inside the definition of a filled polygon.

" Start or end the name of a production.

(Start the name of a macro referenced in a production.

) End the name of a macro referenced in a production.

Turtle Geometry in Three Dimensions

In the two prior sections our turtle was crawling along the ground, its movements restricted to a plane. Now our turtle is flying through the air and oblivious to the normal rules of aerodynamics, able to fly straight up, or upside-down, or in any other orientation, with its only restriction being that it always flies *forward*, whatever direction forward may be at the time.

When the turtle is confined to a plane, only left and right turns are possible, and they are well defined. But now consider a flying turtle. Suppose it is in the 'usual' orientation, belly-side down, and pointing north. Then if it makes a 90 degree left turn it will still be belly-side down and now pointing west. But suppose it had been flying upside-down, with its back toward the ground. Now a left turn will cause it to point east, though still with its back to the ground. Or suppose it had been flying with its right side toward the ground. Now a left turn will cause it to point straight up, with its tail pointing toward the ground. So we see that the effect of a turn depends on its orientation at the time it turned.

It is useful to define the turtle's orientation by means of three mutually perpendicular direction vectors. We will be working in a 3D coordinate system. For our purposes we will assume that this coordinate system has the +X axis pointing to our right, the +Y axis pointing directly away from us, and the +Z axis pointing straight up. Thus, we are looking at the turtle from infinitely far out on the −Y axis.

The three direction vectors (which for mathematical convenience we assume are unit length) that define the turtle's orientation are:

H   The heading of the turtle, the direction it is pointing and hence the direction in which it moves when it takes a step forward.

U   Up, the direction which the turtle perceives as being up. Its back is facing in this direction. Note that this need not be 'up' for the observer. For example, if the turtle happens to be flying upside-down as we see it, its 'up' will be pointing in the −Z direction.

L   Left, the direction that the turtle perceives as being to its left.

A little thought should tell us that any two of these three directions are sufficient to define the orientation of the turtle. In fact, these directions are related by the *cross-product* operation, abbreviated with the symbol ×; If you know any two, you can compute the third. In particular, $L=H \times U$. This cross product operation is defined in Equation (5.1), in which U_X stands for the X coordinate of U and so forth.

$$
\begin{aligned}
L_X &= U_Y * H_Z - U_Z * H_Y \\
L_Y &= U_Z * H_X - U_X * H_Z \\
L_Z &= U_X * H_Y - U_Y * H_X
\end{aligned}
\tag{5.1}
$$

We are now equipped to rigorously describe the three types of rotations the turtle can do: turn left/right, pitch up/down, and roll left/right. Each of these three rotations is done about one of the three direction vectors just defined:

Turn left/right is rotation about the U (Up) vector.
Pitch up/down is rotation about the L (Left) vector.
Roll left/right is rotation about the H (Heading) vector.

When we rotate about a direction vector, that vector does not change; only the other two vectors change. For example, if we turn left, U does not change; up is still the same up direction. Rotation about a direction vector can be generalized as follows. Let V be some vector we wish to rotate, and let P be a vector perpendicular to it. We want to rotate V around the vector that is perpendicular to both of them, $V \times P$. This is done as shown in Equation (5.2), where V' is V after rotation by the angle θ. Mathematically inclined readers should be able to confirm this with a sketch, while others may wish to consult any standard 3D graphics textbook.

$$
V' = \cos(\theta) V + \sin(\theta) P
\tag{5.2}
$$

In order to rigorously define the direction of rotation (left vs right, up vs down) we need to be careful about the sign of the rotation angle. The correct equations for our turtle rotations are shown on the next page. They are just specific instances of Equation (5.2) In these equations, turning or rolling left, and pitching up, correspond to a positive rotation angle.

Since any two direction vectors define the third, we follow the common convention of maintaining the heading vector H and the up vector U, and use the relation $L=H \times U$ as shown in Equation (5.1) to get the left vector L whenever we need it. Observe that when we change the pitch, both of our preserved vectors H and U change, so we have to update both. When programming the two parts of Equation (5.5) one must be careful to preserve the pre-rotation values of H to use in the second equation; do not use the rotated H from the first equation to compute the second equation.

$$H_{Yaw}(\theta) \ = \ \cos(\theta)\,H \ + \ \sin(\theta)\,L \qquad\qquad (5.3)$$

$$H_{Roll}(\theta) \ = \ \cos(\theta)\,U \ + \ \sin(\theta)\,L \qquad\qquad (5.4)$$

$$\begin{aligned} H_{Pitch}(\theta) \ &= \ \cos(\theta)\,H \ + \ \sin(\theta)\,U \\ U_{Pitch}(\theta) \ &= \ \cos(\theta)\,U \ + \ \sin(\theta)\,H \end{aligned} \qquad\qquad (5.5)$$

To take a step forward we just add to the current position the required distance times the heading H. In other words, let *Position* be the current (x, y, z) location of the turtle. If we want to move forward a distance D, our updated position is given by Equation (5.6). Recall that H, L, and U are all unit length.

$$\textit{New position} \ = \ \textit{Position} \ + \ D * H \qquad\qquad (5.6)$$

A Note on Filled Polygons

When we want to draw plant parts such as leaves or flowers it is essential to have the ability to draw filled polygons. To facilitate this, *LIN* has two different step sizes. These are the standard unit step size for forward (command F) motion, and a generally smaller S size used to map out the border of a filled polygon. We'll explore this in more detail later. For now, know that this path is defined by commands enclosed in curly braces {}, and that the turtle status is pushed onto the stack before the border path is defined, and then restored from the stack when the border is complete.

Algorithm for Moving the Turtle

This section presents in great detail the complete algorithm for converting the 3D turtle commands listed on Page 107 into the string of (x, y, z) coordinates of the turtle's path. Complete C++ source code for this algorithm is in the turtle() routine in the source file COMPUTE_3DAG.CPP. The following parameters are supplied by the user in advance:

angle   The turning angle in degrees, 0-90. If right angles will be an essential part of the motion, this should be an integer division of 90, such as 22.5 degrees.

width   The initial width of the lines that delineate the turtle's path, in pixels. If this is not odd it will be bumped up to the next odd number.

stepsize   Used for tracing the border of a filled object, this is the fraction of the initial forward motion distance accomplished by the *F* command. This controls the size of filled polygons relative to the size of the complete figure. In most cases the appropriate value will depend on the number of iterations, with more iterations requiring larger values.

shrink   This is the multiplier (virtually always 1 or less) for the line thickness used each time the *V* (shrink) command is executed.

The algorithm, shown on the next page, begins with initializations. The sine and cosine of the turning angle will be needed so often that we precompute them. We will always maintain current values for the drawing thickness and color, the turtle's position, heading *H*, and up *U*. We keep track of the minimum and maximum values of its position so we can rescale the path later. The path will be saved in the x, y, and z output vectors, which are indexed by node. The turtle always starts at the position (0, 0, 0), which is the first 'computed' node. The stack pointer is initialized to zero (nothing on the stack). There are n user-defined operations in opstr, and these will define the turtle's path.

```
cos_a = cos ( PI * angle / 180.0 )              Must convert degrees to radians
sin_a = sin ( PI * angle / 180.0 )
current_thickness = width
current_color = 0
current_x = current_y = current_z = 0.0    Position of turtle
current_hx = current_hy = 0.0               Heading H
current_hz = 1.0
current_ux = current_uz = 0.0               Up U
current_uy = -1.0


xmin = ymin = zmin = 1.e30                  Boundary of the complete path
xmax = ymax = zmax = -1.e30


x[0] = y[0] = z[0] = 0.0                     Path starts here
node = 1                                     Index into node arrays
kstack = 0                                   Number of items on stack


For i from 0 through n-1                     Do each command in op string


  left_x = current_uy * current_hz - current_uz * current_hy    Eq (5.1)
  left_y = current_uz * current_hx - current_ux * current_hz
  left_z = current_ux * current_hy - current_uy * current_hx


  If opstr[i] = P_FORWARD                   Take a step forward (F)
    current_x = current_x + current_hx      Equation (5.6)
    current_y = current_y + current_hy      Step distance=1 by definition
    current_z = current_z + current_hz
    if (current_x < xmin)                   Keep track of path's extent
      xmin = current_x
    if (current_x > xmax)
      xmax = current_x
    if (current_y < ymin)
      ymin = current_y
    if (current_y > ymax)
      ymax = current_y
    if (current_z < zmin)
      zmin = current_z
    if (current_z > zmax)
      zmax = current_z
    x[node] = current_x                     Save path in output
    y[node] = current_y
    z[node] = current_z
    thickness[node] = current_thickness  Also save thickness and color
    draw_line[node] = current_color + 1
    node = node + 1
```

Else If opstr[i] = P_STEP   *Small step forward for filled outline*
current_x = current_x + stepsize * current_hx   *Equation (5.6)*
current_y = current_y + stepsize * current_hy
current_z = current_z + stepsize * current_hz
if (current_x < xmin)   *Keep track of path's extent*
 xmin = current_x
if (current_x > xmax)
 xmax = current_x
if (current_y < ymin)
 ymin = current_y
if (current_y > ymax)
 ymax = current_y
if (current_z < zmin)
 zmin = current_z
if (current_z > zmax)
 zmax = current_z
x[node] = current_x   *Save path in output*
y[node] = current_y
z[node] = current_z
draw_line[node] = -(current_color + 1)   *Negative flags filled polygon*
node = node + 1

Else If opstr[i] = P_PLUS   *Turn left*
current_hx = current_hx * cos_a + left_x * sin_a   *Equation (5.3)*
current_hy = current_hy * cos_a + left_y * sin_a
current_hz = current_hz * cos_a + left_z * sin_a

Else If opstr[i] = P_MINUS   *Turn right*
current_hx = current_hx * cos_a - left_x * sin_a   *Equation (5.3)*
current_hy = current_hy * cos_a - left_y * sin_a
current_hz = current_hz * cos_a - left_z * sin_a

Else If opstr[i] = P_ROLL_LEFT   *Roll left*
current_ux = current_ux * cos_a + left_x * sin_a   *Equation (5.4)*
current_uy = current_uy * cos_a + left_y * sin_a
current_uz = current_uz * cos_a + left_z * sin_a

Else If opstr[i] = P_ROLL_RIGHT   *Equation (5.4)*
current_ux = current_ux * cos_a - left_x * sin_a
current_uy = current_uy * cos_a - left_y * sin_a
current_uz = current_uz * cos_a - left_z * sin_a

```
Else If opstr[i] = P_PITCH_UP                    Pitch up
  tx = current_hx                                Equation (5.5)
  ty = current_hy
  tz = current_hz
  current_hx = current_hx * cos_a + current_ux * sin_a
  current_hy = current_hy * cos_a + current_uy * sin_a
  current_hz = current_hz * cos_a + current_uz * sin_a
  current_ux = current_ux * cos_a - tx * sin_a
  current_uy = current_uy * cos_a - ty * sin_a
  current_uz = current_uz * cos_a - tz * sin_a

Else If opstr[i] = P_PITCH_DOWN                  Pitch down
  tx = current_hx                                Equation (5.5)
  ty = current_hy                                Must save pre-rotate H
  tz = current_hz
  current_hx = current_hx * cos_a - current_ux * sin_a
  current_hy = current_hy * cos_a - current_uy * sin_a
  current_hz = current_hz * cos_a - current_uz * sin_a
  current_ux = current_ux * cos_a + tx * sin_a
  current_uy = current_uy * cos_a + ty * sin_a
  current_uz = current_uz * cos_a + tz * sin_a

Else If opstr[i] = P_TURN_AROUND         Turn around (heading 180)
  current_hx = -current_hx
  current_hy = -current_hy
  current_hz = -current_hz

Else If opstr[i] = P_SHRINK                       Shrink line thickness
  current_thickness = current_thickness *  shrink
  If current_thickness < 1.0
    current_thickness = 1.0

else if opstr[i] = P_COLOR                        Set line color
  i = i + 1
  current_color = opstr[i]
```

```
Else If opstr[i] = P_PUSH  OR  opstr[i] = P_START_BRACE
    stack_x[kstack] = current_x          Push state onto stack
    stack_y[kstack] = current_y
    stack_z[kstack] = current_z
    stack_hx[kstack] = current_hx
    stack_hy[kstack] = current_hy
    stack_hz[kstack] = current_hz
    stack_ux[kstack] = current_ux
    stack_uy[kstack] = current_uy
    stack_uz[kstack] = current_uz
    stack_t[kstack] = current_thickness
    stack_c[kstack] = current_color
    kstack = kstack + 1

Else If opstr[i] = P_POP  OR  opstr[i] = P_END_BRACE
    kstack = kstack - 1                   Pop state from stack
    current_x = stack_x[kstack]
    current_y = stack_y[kstack]
    current_z = stack_z[kstack]
    current_hx = stack_hx[kstack]
    current_hy = stack_hy[kstack]
    current_hz = stack_hz[kstack]
    current_ux = stack_ux[kstack]
    current_uy = stack_uy[kstack]
    current_uz = stack_uz[kstack]
    current_thickness = stack_t[kstack]
    current_color = stack_c[kstack]
    x[node] = current_x                  Move turtle to restored place
    y[node] = current_y
    z[node] = current_z
    No need to put thickness in node because no line drawn; just moved
    draw_line[node] = 0       Flag that no line is to be drawn; just move
    node = node + 1

Else If opstr[i] = P_NAME   Production name does nothing to turtle
    i = i + 1                            Must bypass index of production
```

End of loop that does all operations

That P_NAME operation requires a comment. In virtually all practical applications the operation string contains production names, placeholders that are replaced by productions as iteration proceeds. This will be discussed in detail later. For now, know that they do not affect the turtle.

At this point the nodes are completely computed and saved. But the turtle likely has wandered far and wide, probably asymmetrically, possibly even below its starting point! Shift and scale the turtle path so that its minimum value is zero in all three dimensions, it never exceeds one in any dimension, and it reaches one in at least one dimension. This preserves the correct aspect ratio while confining the path to a known volume, a property that makes display later a lot easier.

```
If xmax-xmin >= ymax-ymin  AND  xmax-xmin >= zmax-zmin
   scale = 1.0 / (xmax - xmin + 1.e-30)
Else If ymax-ymin >= xmax-xmin  AND  ymax-ymin >= zmax-zmin
   scale = 1.0 / (ymax - ymin + 1.e-30)
Else       zmax-zmin >= xmax-xmin  AND  zmax-zmin >= ymax-ymin
   scale = 1.0 / (zmax - zmin + 1.e-30)

For i From 0 Through node-1
   x[i] = scale * (x[i] - xmin)
   y[i] = scale * (y[i] - ymin)
   z[i] = scale * (z[i] - zmin)

return node            Tell the caller how many nodes were computed
```

Rotating the Turtle's Path for Display

Although the turtle moves about in three dimensions, most of the time we will have only two dimensions available for display, such as a computer monitor or printed page. We have to collapse out one dimension. The convention that I (and most others) chose is to view the turtle from infinitely far out on the –Y axis, with +X pointing to the right and +Z pointing up. As in the prior section, the default starting orientation of the turtle is straight up (+Z), as a plant would normally grow, and with –X being its left direction. Thus, we begin with $H=(0, 0, 1)$, $U=(0, -1, 0)$, and $L=(-1, 0, 0)$. This leads to a natural default viewing method: ignore the Y coordinate of the turtle and plot its path using its X coordinate as the horizontal viewing axis (+X to the right) and its Z coordinate as the vertical viewing axis (+Z up).

It would, however, be a grievous limitation if we could view the turtle's path from only straight-on at ground level. We would like to be able to look at the path from all around, and at elevations above ground level. As is often the case in 3D applications, rather than moving the eye it is easier to rotate the object while keeping the eye at its location infinitely far out on the –Y axis.

The user will specify two quantities that control the viewing position:

Azimuth (Az) is the counterclockwise rotation of the eye around the Z axis, in the range 0-360 degrees. To accomplish this we actually rotate the turtle's path in a clockwise direction.

Elevation (El) is the elevation in the range 0-90 degrees of the eye above the XY plane. To accomplish this we rotate the turtle's path downward.

Although there are formulas for performing both operations simultaneously, I find it easier to do each separately. First I rotate it *Az* degrees around the Z axis, and then I rotate it *El* degrees around the X axis. At this point it will be viewed at the correct azimuth and elevation if we look at the path from infinitely far out the –Y axis.

The azimuth rotation is accomplished with Equation (5.7), and the elevation with Equation (5.8).

$$x' = \cos(Az)x + \sin(Az)y$$
$$y' = \cos(Az)y - \sin(Az)x \tag{5.7}$$

$$y' = \cos(El)y - \sin(El)z$$
$$z' = \cos(El)z + \sin(El)y \tag{5.8}$$

After rotation we need to rescale the 2D projection to fit the view frame. Earlier we rescaled it to the range 0-1, but here we will scale it to be very slightly smaller than this so that thick lines do not go outside the view frame. Also, the earlier scaling needed to keep the correct aspect ratio in all three dimensions, but since we will be displaying path positions based only on the X (right-left) and Z (up-down) coordinates we need to scale only those dimensions. We do need to compute the rotated Y coordinates, because we will need them for hidden line/surface elimination later. But it is pointless to take them into account for scaling limits, as their later use will depend only on ordering, not magnitude. Here is the rotation algorithm:

```
sine_azimuth = sin ( PI * azimuth / 180.0 )
cosine_azimuth = cos ( PI *azimuth / 180.0 )
sine_elevation = sin ( PI * elevation / 180.0 )
cosine_elevation = cos ( PI * elevation / 180.0 )

For i from 0 Through n–1

    First, rotate clockwise about Z, because the eye rotates CCW
    tempval = x[i]              Equation (5.7)
    x[i] = cosine_azimuth * x[i] + sine_azimuth * y[i]
    y[i] = cosine_azimuth * y[i] - sine_azimuth * tempval

    Now rotate downward about X, because the eye rises above XY plane
    tempval = y[i]              Equation (5.8)
    y[i] = cosine_elevation * y[i] - sine_elevation * z[i]
    z[i] = cosine_elevation * z[i] + sine_elevation * tempval
```

Find the range in all dimensions, though we don't really need Y

```
xmin = ymin = zmin = 1.e30        Boundary of the figure
xmax = ymax = zmax = -1.e30

For i From 0 Through n-1
  If x[i] < xmin
    xmin = x[i]
  If x[i] > xmax
    xmax = x[i]
  If y[i] < ymin
    ymin = y[i]
  If y[i] > ymax
    ymax = y[i]
  If z[i] < zmin
    zmin = z[i]
  If z[i] > zmax
    zmax = z[i]
  }
```

The nodes are rotated. Shift and scale them based on X and Z only.

```
If xmax-xmin >= zmax-zmin
  scale = 0.98 / (xmax - xmin + 1.e-30)
Else
  scale = 0.98 / (zmax - zmin + 1.e-30)

For i From 0 Through n-1
  x[i] = scale * (x[i] - xmin) + 0.01
  y[i] = scale * (y[i] - ymin) + 0.01
  z[i] = scale * (z[i] - zmin) + 0.01
```

Note that we really don't need to bother with scaling Y, but I do it anyway to facilitate later modifications that someone might do, such as perspective plots.

Complete C++ source code for the algorithm just shown is in the routine rotate_image() in source file COMPUTE_3DAG.CPP.

Building the Image

The routine build_image() in source file COMPUTE_3DAG.CPP takes the output of the algorithm just shown and converts it to a full-color image. It uses the tediously long Bresenham algorithm for drawing lines, so the complete algorithm cannot be shown here. However, this outline should make clear the additions needed for the Bresenham algorithm to handle 3D issues such as hidden line/surface elimination and filling in polygons. Rather than breaking up the algorithm and separately analyzing each, it is more clear to just present the algorithm in its entirety and then walk through it afterward.

This algorithm, shown on the next page, has three major differences/additions compared to the image building algorithm MakeImage() shown in the prior section for 2D axial generation (Page 105).

- There, the flag array draw_line created by the turtle() routine was strictly binary: do we draw a line connecting the prior point to the current point, or do we just move without drawing a line. But this array has two additional uses here. Its sign is meaningful, with positive indicating that we are doing ordinary forward moves (the *F* command), and negative indicating that we are doing *S* steps to outline the boundary of a filled polygon. Also, its absolute value in the range 1-10 indicates which of up to ten user-specified colors will be used for the line.

- The nrows by ncols fill_buffer matrix, created and used only in this routine, is used when a filled polygon is defined. The perimeter of the polygon, including distance, is written to this matrix, and when the polygon definition concludes, the pixels inside the boundaries are set.

- The nrows by ncols z_buffer matrix, created and used only in this routine, keeps track of the distance (the Y coordinate) separating the eye from the closest path part that happens to appear in each pixel. The first time a path part appears in a pixel, its Y coordinate is put into this matrix. Thereafter, only path parts that are closer than the closest so far are written to the image. This allows nearby parts to hide more distant parts.

Initialize image to all white
Initialize fill_buffer and z_buffer to infinitely distant from the eye

xa = Round (ncols * x[0])
ya = Round (nrows * y[0])

For node from 1 through Nnodes–1
  xb = Round (ncols * x[node])
  yb = Round (nrows * y[node])

  If draw_line[node] = 0

    If we just drew a filled object, this is the POP due to closing curly brace.
    Fill in the object and then zero the fill buffer to get ready for the next.
    If draw_line[node-1] < 0   *Prior node was perimeter of a filled polygon?*
        color = -(draw_line[node-1] + 1)   *Get the predefined color ID*
        For i From 0 Through nrows-1 *Check all rows for filled polygon*
          k = 0   *Will count perimeter flags in this row*
          first = last = -1

          For j From 0 Through ncols-1
            If fill_buffer[i*ncols+j] < 1.e59   *Is this a boundary node?*
              k = k + 1   *Count perimeter flags*
              If first < 0
                first = j
                first_dist = fill_buffer[i*ncols+j]
              last = j
              last_dist = fill_buffer[i*ncols+j]
          End of For j loop, scanning columns for first and last perimeter

          If k < 2
            Continue i (row) loop by skipping remaining code inside loop

          We now assume k=2: the user has a convex polygon
          For j From first Through last *Fill interior in this row, interpolating*
            distance = first_dist + (last_dist-first_dist) * (j - first) / (last - first)
            If distance < z_buffer[i*ncols+j]   *Is this node visible?*
              z_buffer[i*ncols+j] = distance   *Update distance to this*
              Set image[row,col] to color   *Implementation dependent*
          End of j (column) loop from first through last
        End of i loop checking all rows

Zero fill buffer to prepare for next object
For i From 0 Through nrows-1
   For j from 0 Through ncols-1
      fill_buffer[i*ncols+j] = 1.e60   *Flag that no boundary here*
End of code block "Prior node was perimeter of a filled polygon"

xa = xb ;
ya = yb ;
Continue to top of node loop, skipping remaining loop code
End of "If draw_line[node] = 0", meaning that we just move due to] or }

*If we get here we are to draw a line from prior node a to this node b
using the Bresenham algorithm, stepping a total of step_dist pixels
from start to finish.*

rate = (y[node] - y[node-1]) / (step_dist + 1.e-20) *For Z buffer*
offset = y[node-1]   *Lets us compute distance along line*

For each (row,col) pixel from (xa, ya) through (xb, yb) (Bresenham)
   distance = offset + (this - start) * rate *Relative distance from eye*
   If draw_line[node] < 0 *Drawing a filled object with 'S'? Flag perimeter*
      fill_buffer[row*ncols+col] = distance *We'll check z_buffer when fill*
   If distance < z_buffer[row*ncols+col]
      z_buffer[row*ncols+col] = distance
      Set image[row,col] to color   *Implementation dependent*
End of Bresenham algorithm, drawing line from a to b

xa = xb
ya = yb
End of node loop, processing all turtle nodes

We begin by setting (xa, ya) to the first node (rounded to the nearest
integer), and then we loop through the remaining nodes. With each pass
through this loop, (xb, yb) will be the current node and (xa, ya) the prior
node. According to the value of draw_line[node] we will either draw a line
connecting these nodes, or we will just move to the new location without
drawing a line. The latter happens when the current point came from
popping the stack, whether from an ordinary closing bracket], or
termination of the boundary of a filled polygon, a curly brace }.

The first thing we do in the node loop is check this very thing. If draw_line[node] is zero either it's just a simple stack pop from], or it's the much more complex situation of ending a filled polygon definition. We make this determination by checking the sign of the prior node's flag, draw_line[node-1]. If it is negative, that prior node was the last node in the perimeter of a filled polygon, so we have to fill it in. Prior to this polygon being defined, all elements of fill_buffer had been initialized to 1.60 as flags that there is no polygon. While the polygon was defined, fill_buffer pixels were set to the corresponding z_buffer distance, as will be seen later in this code. So right now fill_buffer will have the perimeter of the polygon set to much smaller values while all other elements remain at 1.e60. This defines the outline of the polygon.

To fill it in we pass through each row of fill_buffer. For each row, find the first and last columns that are flagged as perimeter pixels. Usually there will be exactly two of them. If there is just one then the user's polygon has a one-pixel-wide 'tail' which does not need filling in. If there are more than two we either have a top or bottom edge, or the user has created a concave polygon, which is not currently legal. The concavity will also be filled in (to the user's dismay).

As we pass from the first through last columns we interpolate to find the distance of each pixel from the eye. This distance is compared to the 'closest so far' in z_buffer. If this one is closer than the closest so far we update that closest distance and set this pixel to the appropriate color, an implementation-dependent operation. But if it's not closer it is hidden by something closer and hence is not displayed. After the entire polygon is filled in we re-initialize fill_buffer to flag that there is no polygon present.

Regardless of whether this was a filled polygon or the much simpler ordinary pop, we make the current node be the prior node for the next iteration and skip over the remaining code in the node loop; that remaining skipped code draws a line, which we do not want to do now.

Computation of the interpolation constants **rate** and **offset** is difficult to make explicit in this outline because the exact nature of this computation depends on the Bresenham line-drawing algorithm. The bottom line is that the algorithm will be stepping one pixel at a time in either the horizontal or vertical direction, whichever has more steps in the total line extent. We need to be able to interpolate the distance from the eye of each pixel along the line. Recall that for the nodes, their X coordinate will be the horizontal location, and their Z coordinate the vertical. Their Y coordinate is the depth, the distance from the eye. So we divide the total depth change from the line start to the line end by the number of steps the algorithm will take. This is the rate of depth change per step. The offset is the depth at the first pixel in the line. This lets us compute by linear interpolation the depth for each pixel along the line.

When we process a pixel, we first see if this node is part of the definition of a filled polygon. If so, put this pixel's depth in fill_buffer to be ready for later when the polygon is filled. Then we compare this distance to the 'closest so far' in z_buffer. If this is now the closest, we update z_buffer and color the pixel.

After the line is completely drawn we make the current pixel be the prior pixel for the next iteration and advance to the next node.

In case you are wondering why even though the depth is in Y we still call the depth array the z_buffer, it's because this term is an industry standard. The depth buffer is *always* called a Z buffer, regardless of where the distance information came from. This is because in most other applications we plot X and Y, using Z for depth. But since we are looking at plants, which grow up from the ground, I find it more intuitive to do it the way I do. Put your complaints in the box by the door.

Iterative Expansion of Operation Strings

If you are not already familiar with the edge replacement and axial generation concepts introduced in the first two main sections of this chapter, you will have a difficult time following the presentation to come. I will for the most part assume knowledge of those ideas and simply expand them to three dimensions and the requisite additional operations.

The overall flow of the process is almost identical to what we've seen before. The idea is that every time we perform an iterative expansion, a *predecessor* string is expanded to the *successor* string by replacing edges and/or productions with user-defined productions. This process begins with the *axiom* and proceeds a user-specified number of times. When iteration has occurred as many times as desired, the operations are converted to turtle moves, which are then displayed. Any references to productions in the final string are ignored by the turtle. This process is shown below.

```
Successor = Axiom
Repeat Depth times
    Predecessor = Successor
    Successor = Expand ( Predecessor )
TurtleMoves = Turtle ( Successor )
Rotated = Rotate ( TurtleMoves )
Image = BuildImage ( Rotated )
```

In my *LIN* implementation, most operations require a single integer to identify the operation. There are only two exceptions. The *Color* command (C) requires a second integer to identify which of up to ten user-defined colors is to be used. And a named production requires a second integer to identify which of the possibly many user-defined productions is being referenced.

The simple edge replacement and axial generation algorithms presented in the first two main section of this chapter allowed at most two different productions, the primary and the secondary. This 3D version of axial generation allows a large number (currently up to 64) of named user-defined productions. In addition, it allows a basic edge-replacement production (ERP) which, if defined, replaces every instance of the *Forward* command (F) with that defined production. Finally, it implements *stochastic generation* by allowing multiple definitions of named productions, associating probabilities with each variation. During iterative expansion, each variety of each named production is randomly selected according to the user-supplied probabilities. This lets the user create entire fields of plants, each of which is structurally similar but not identical.

The expansion algorithm is shown below. Complete source code for it is in the advance() routine in COMPUTE_3DAG.CPP. In this algorithm, j++ means that j is incremented *after* the line is executed, while ++i means that i is incremented *before* the line is executed. There are nops elements in the source array. The optional *edge replacement production*, if any, is in erp and it contains n_erp elements. Production id has prod_nrand[id] different random variations, with prod_prob[id][m] being the *cumulative* probability of variation m. This variation has prod_nops[id][m] elements in its definition string, and this string is pointed to by prod_ops[id][m]. Here is the algorithm, and a short discussion follows.

```
j = 0

For i From 0 Through nops-1
  If source[i] = P_PLUS
    dest[j++] = P_PLUS
  Else If source[i] = P_MINUS
    dest[j++] = P_MINUS
  Else If source[i] = P_PUSH
    dest[j++] = P_PUSH
  Else If source[i] = P_POP
    dest[j++] = P_POP
  Else If source[i] = P_START_BRACE
    dest[j++] = P_START_BRACE
  Else If source[i] = P_END_BRACE
    dest[j++] = P_END_BRACE
  Else If source[i] = P_SHRINK
    dest[j++] = P_SHRINK
  Else If source[i] = P_STEP
    dest[j++] = P_STEP
  Else If source[i] = P_PITCH_DOWN
    dest[j++] = P_PITCH_DOWN
  Else If source[i] = P_PITCH_UP
    dest[j++] = P_PITCH_UP
```

```
Else If source[i] = P_ROLL_LEFT
  dest[j++] = P_ROLL_LEFT
Else If source[i] = P_ROLL_RIGHT
  dest[j++] = P_ROLL_RIGHT
Else If source[i] = P_TURN_AROUND
  dest[j++] = P_TURN_AROUND

Else If source[i] = P_COLOR
  dest[j++] = P_COLOR
  dest[j++] = source[++i]        The selected color, 0-9

Else If source[i] = P_FORWARD
  If params->erp = NULL
    dest[j++] = P_FORWARD
  Else
    For k From 0 Through n_erp-1
      dest[j++] = params->erp[k]

Else If source[i] = P_NAME
  id = source[++i]          Index of the named production
  ff = uniform_random()     Generate 0 <= random < 1
  For m From 0 Through prod_nrand[id]-1
    If ff <= prod_prob[id][m]
      break out of loop      We just randomly selected version m
  For k From 0 Through prod_nops[id][m]
    dest[j++] = prod_ops[id][m][k]   Insert this production

return j ;
```

Most operations are simply copied from the source to the destination. The *Color* operation needs the color id copied as well. If there is no *edge replacement production*, the *Forward* command is just copied. But if there is an ERP, it replaces the *Forward* command.

A named production requires that we generate a random number to select m, the index of the variation to be used. Prior to this routine being called, the user-specified probabilities have been summed to make them a cumulative distribution function. For example, (0.3, 0.6, 0.1) would be changed to (0.3, 0.9, 1.0). We then insert that production into the slot that contained the name.

3D Axial Generation in the LIN Program

When the user clicks *Image / 3D Axial Growth*, a file selection dialog will appear, allowing the user the read a definition file. If such a file has not yet been read, it must be read before proceeding. If a definition file has already been read, the user may click *Cancel* to keep the existing definition. A second dialog then appears, shown in Figure 5.19.

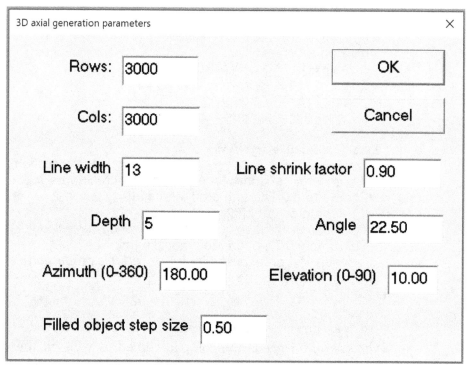

Figure 5.19: 3D Axial Generation dialog

All of the items in this dialog can be set in the definition file, and any changes made to them in this dialog supercede values in the definition file. The usual process is to read a definition file and then run the generation multiple times without rereading a definition file, varying parameters set in the dialog shown above. The definition of all possible commands in the definition file is now shown, along with the syntax. Each command occupies a single line.

NROWS Number

Specifies the number of rows in the generated image. It is strongly recommended that this equal the number of columns so that correct aspect ratio is preserved if a file is written. For printing, a good rule of thumb is to use at least 300 pixels per inch.

NCOLS Number

Specifies the number of columns in the generated image.

ANGLE Number

Specifies the fixed angle in degrees (0-90) for orientation changes. If the generated object ever requires right angles, this should be an integer division of 90, such as 30 or 22.5.

WIDTH Number

Specifies the width of lines drawn in pixels. If an even number is specified it is incremented to make it odd.

DEPTH Number

Specifies the number of iterative expansions. If this is zero, no expansion is done and only the Axiom is processed.

SHRINK Number

Specifies the multiplier (0-1) by which the line width is reduced each time the *V* command is encountered.

STEP Number

Specifies the multiplier (usually but not necessarily less than one) of the original forward step size (*F*) to be used for outlining the perimeter of filled polygons. In most cases this will have to be increased as the number of iterations increases. This is because as we iterate, in most applications the initial forward step size decreases relative to the overall image size.

AZIMUTH Number

Specifies the counterclockwise rotation of the eye around the Z axis, in the range 0-360 degrees.

ELEVATION Number

Specifies the elevation in the range 0-90 degrees of the eye above the XY plane.

COLOR Red Green Blue

Defines a color for lines. Each of the three numbers must be an integer in the range 0 (none of this color present) to 255 (maximum possible presence of this color). Later, when colors are specified with the *C#* command, that command will refer to the ordinal number of the specified colors, starting at 0. So color 0 is the first color defined, color 1 is the second, and so forth. At most ten colors can be defined.

MACRO "Name" Commands

This allows the user to simplify definitions by associating a descriptive name with a frequently used command string. When a production or the axiom is defined, the user can enclose a macro name in parentheses. That macro's command string will then be substituted for the parenthesized name. Maximum name length is 15 characters and cannot contain spaces or special characters, only letters and numbers. It is not case sensitive. For example, one might define MACRO "HardLeft" ++++ so that in later commands the string ++++ will be inserted in place of any encounter with (HardLeft).

AXIOM Commands

This mandatory definition line specifies the command string for the axiom.

ERP Commands

This optional definition line specifies a special production, the *Edge Replacement Production*. For each iteration of expansion, this command string replaces every instance of the Forward (*F*) command.

PRODUCTION "Name" Commands
PRODUCTION <Probability> "Name" Commands

The Production command, optional but with at least one nearly always present, specifies the production(s) to be used for iterative expansion. If more than one production with the same name is specified, the user must include for each a probability enclosed in angle brackets. For clarity these probabilities must sum to one, although if they do not they will be automatically normalized to do so.

The production commands were listed in summary form at the start of this main section on Page 107. We reproduce this command set here, but with more detail now.

F Take a step forward in the direction of the current heading. Orientation does not change. The step size remains fixed throughout iterations, although in most applications the distance traveled by the turtle increases with each iteration, meaning that the size of a step relative to the fixed image size decreases.

+ Turn left. In aeronautics this is called *yaw*. Rotation is around the Up vector. This adds the fixed angle to the current heading.

− Turn right. Rotation is around the Up vector. This subtracts the fixed angle from the current heading.

^ Pitch up, as in an airplane taking off. Rotation is around the Left vector. This adds the fixed angle to the current pitch.

& Pitch down, as in an airplane diving toward the ground. Rotation is around the Left vector. This subtracts the fixed angle from the current pitch.

**** Roll left, as in an airplane dipping its left wing down and right wing up. Rotation is around the Heading vector.

/ Roll right. Rotation is around the Heading vector.

| Turn around (reverse direction). This is a 180 degree rotation around the Up vector.

V Shrink the diameter of the cylinder (line after projection) being drawn by the turtle's path. The current thickness is multiplied by the fixed Shrink constant, but not allowed to become less than one.

[Push the current turtle state onto a stack. The state includes the turtle's position, Heading, Up direction, line thickness, and color.

] Pop the stack to restore the turtle state.

C# Set the color to one of ten choices, where # is a digit from 0 through 9. Color 0 refers to the first color defined in the definition file, 1 the second color, and so forth.

{ Start definition of a filled polygon, and push state onto stack. The polygon always lies strictly on the plane perpendicular to the Up vector, so its perimeter is defined by moving and changing the Heading. The only operations allowed inside curly brackets are S (step forward by the fixed STEP size), + (turn left by the fixed angle), – (turn right) and | (reverse direction).

} End definition of filled polygon and pop state from stack.

S Take a step inside the definition of a filled polygon. The size of this step is defined by the STEP command and is usually but not necessarily less than 1. The ordinary step forward command *F* has a step size of 1 by definition.

" Start or end the name of a production, or the name of a macro when the macro is defined. When a production is defined its name must be enclosed in quotes, and whenever a production is referenced in the axiom or a production its name must also be enclosed in quotes. When a macro is referenced in the axiom or a production its name must be enclosed in parentheses.

(Start the name of a macro when it is referenced in the axiom or a production. When a macro is defined its name must be enclosed in quotes (").

) End the name of a macro when it is referenced in the axiom or a production.

Here are some examples of lines or sets of lines that might be found in a definition file, along with a description of their effects.

-------------------------------> **Example 1** <----------------------------

```
ANGLE 20
AXIOM F
ERP [+F] [-F] FF
```

This simple example has an axiom that does nothing but take a single step forward. There are no named productions, only an edge replacement production. The command string after the first and then the second iteration are as shown below, and the path is shown in Figure 5.20.

[+F] [-F] FF   *First iteration*
[+[+F][-F]FF] [-[+F][-F]FF] [+F] [-F] FF [+F] [-F] FF   *Second iteration*

The reader should verify that the command string for the second iteration is obtained by substituting the ERP for every occurrence of *F* in the first iteration's string. Let's walk through the first few moves:
1) Push the state on the stack and turn left 20 degrees.
2) Push the state and turn left another 20 degrees.
3) Take a step forward. This is the bottom-left line.
4) Pop the state stack, returning to the bottom, pointing left 20 degrees then immediately save the state again.
5) Turn right 20 degrees, pointing up, and take a step.
6) Pop the state stack, returning to the bottom, pointing left 20 degrees. Take two steps. This is the left slanted line, second from the bottom.
7) The next group draws the two bottom-right lines
8) The remainder of the figure is straightforward.

Fig 5.20: Ex 1

-------------------------------> **Example 2** <----------------------------

ANGLE 20
AXIOM "Branch"
PRODUCTION "Branch" "Branch" F [+F] [-F]

This example differs from the prior in two ways. First, instead of using simple ERP edge replacement, it uses a named production. Second, and much more consequential, this production is strictly left recursive (the recursive production appears only on the left), while the prior example used right recursion. This greatly changes the nature of the path, and in general simplifies it. We certainly see simplification here! The takeaway is that when designing a pattern, we should favor strict left recursion whenever possible. The command string after the first, second, and third iterations are shown below, and the path is shown in Figure 5.21.

"BRANCH" F [+F] [-F]   *First iteration*
"BRANCH" F [+F] [-F] F [+F] [-F]   *Second iteration*
"BRANCH" F [+F] [-F] F [+F] [-F] F [+F] [-F]   *Third iteration*

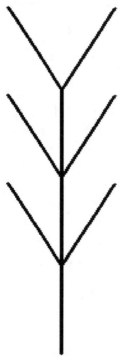

The rule for iteratively expanding the operation string is simple: whenever the production name "Branch" appears, substitute its definition: "Branch" F [+F] [-F]. It's recursive because after expanding, the named production appears, and it's left recursive because it appears on the left. Compare the second iteration here with that in the prior example. Note how right recursion creates expansions that are vastly more complex and difficult to understand than left recursion, even though right recursion is sometimes required.

It bears repeating that when the turtle path is computed, encounters with the production name ("Branch" here) have no impact on the turtle. The operation string interpreter skips right over production names, ignoring them. The only role played by the production name is in iterative expansion.

Fig 5.21: Ex 2

----------------------------> **Example 3** <-----------------------------

```
ANGLE 20
STEP 0.3
AXIOM "Branch"
PRODUCTION <0.5> "Branch"    "Branch" F [+F "Ornament"] [-F]
PRODUCTION <0.5> "Branch"    "Branch" F [+F] [-F "Ornament"]
PRODUCTION "Ornament"        [ {+S --S + | +S --S} ]
```

This example introduces three new concepts: we include two different productions for "Branch" which will be randomly selected at *expansion time* (before turtle movement). We include a second production, "Ornament". And we define the Ornament as a filled polygon. The command string after the first and second iterations are shown below, and the path is shown in Figure 5.22.

```
"BRANCH "F [+F] [-F "ORNAMENT"]
"BRANCH" F [+F] [-F "ORNAMENT"] F [+F] [-F [{+S--S+|+S--S}]]
```

The two definitions of the Branch production differ only in whether the ornament is attached to the left branch or the right branch.

You may wonder why the first pair of branches has no Ornament. The reason should be clear from looking at the command strings above. Early on, when that first pair of branches is drawn, the "Ornament" production, which is not mentioned in the axiom, has not yet been expanded; it's still just a production name that is ignored by the turtle. Only after a second iteration can it be expanded into the filled polygon.

This example also illustrates a common technique for creating a laterally symmetric filled polygon. Do whatever turns and steps that you want to do to define the shape. Finish the first side by performing whatever turns you need to get equal numbers of + and – so you end up pointing directly away from the starting point. Then turn around (|) and repeat the same sequence of turns and steps. This returns you to the starting point.

Fig 5.22: Ex 3

---------------------------------> **Example 4** <----------------------------

```
ANGLE 15
STEP 0.2
DEPTH 5
SHRINK 0.7
COLOR 255 0 0
COLOR 0 255 0
COLOR 0 0 255
MACRO "Ornament" [ {++S ----S ++ | ++S ----S} ]
AXIOM "Plant"
PRODUCTION "Plant" [[C0 "Shoot"] //////// [C1 "Shoot"] //////// [C2 "Shoot"]]
PRODUCTION "Shoot" [&&&FF "Branch" ]
PRODUCTION "Branch" [+VF "Branch" F (Ornament)]
                    [-VF "Branch" F (Ornament)]
```

The prior three examples were all two-dimensional, which may seem rather silly when presenting a three-dimensional technique. Yet they illustrated vital basic concepts without getting into the intricacies of a third dimension. But now we venture into the third dimension. This example also introduces the use of a macro, as well as color just for display clarity.

Note that in the listing above, the Branch production is split over two lines. This is only because the full definition would not fit on one printed line here. This is illegal in the definition file; the entire definition must appear on a single line.

We saw in the prior example that no ornament appeared on the first branch due to the fact that the Ornament production had not yet been expanded into its filled polygon at the time the first branch was drawn. This problem is easily solved by not making Ornament a production, which would require an additional iteration for its expansion. Instead, embed its definition right into the Branch definition so that it is drawn at the same time the branch is drawn. One could simply put its definition in each of the two file lines that define Branch, but its definition is fairly long and would need to be inserted twice (both Branch definitions). The definition file can be made simpler and more clear to anyone reading it, not to mention more maintainable, by making it a macro. When the definition file is compiled, every occurrence of (Ornament) will be replaced by [{++S ----S ++ | ++S ----S}].

The next three lines show the operation strings after the first and second iterations, and the first third of the third iteration.

```
[[C0"SHOOT"]////////[C1"SHOOT"]////////[C2"SHOOT"]]
[[C0[&&&FF"BRANCH"]]////////[C1[&&&FF"BRANCH"]]////////[C2[&&&FF"BRANCH"]]]
[[C0[&&&FF[+F"BRANCH"F[{++S----S++|++S----S}]]][-F"BRANCH"F[{++S----S++|++S----S}]]]////////
```

The first iteration's string does not move the turtle at all. The second draws the three base Shoots (FF three times) and nothing else. It's not until the third iteration that we get branches with ornaments at the end. This third line shows just the first of the three branches; the other two are identical.

It's important to understand how the Shoots are made to radiate outward in three dimensions, because this is a useful technique. A Shoot first pitches down at three times the predefined angle (&&&). It then takes two steps forward in that direction (FF) and spawns a Branch. The Shoot production is enclosed in square brackets [], so when its drawing is complete the turtle will be restored to the position and orientation that it had before the Shoot was drawn.

Now look at the Plant production. After the first Shoot is drawn (colored red for clarity on the display), the turtle's orientation rolls 8 times the angle (////////), which is a total of 120 degrees here. So now when the second Shoot is drawn it will pitch forward in this new, rotated direction.

Finally, let's discuss the Branch. It has two nearly identical parts, each enclosed in square brackets so that after a part is drawn the turtle is restored to its state prior to drawing the part. The first part of the Branch turns slightly left (+), shrinks the line width (V), takes a step (F), and recursively draws another Branch. After that Branch is drawn it takes a single step forward (F) and draws an ornament at the end of that line segment. Then it restores the turtle's status and repeats the process, except that this time it begins with a right turn instead of a left turn.

Front and top views of this object are shown in Figures 5.23 and 5.24 on the next page.

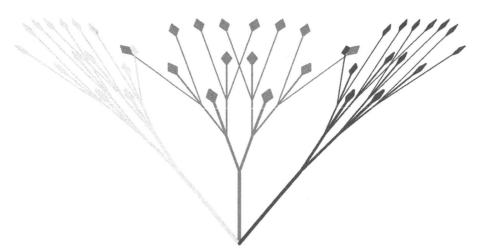

Figure 5.23: Example 4, front view

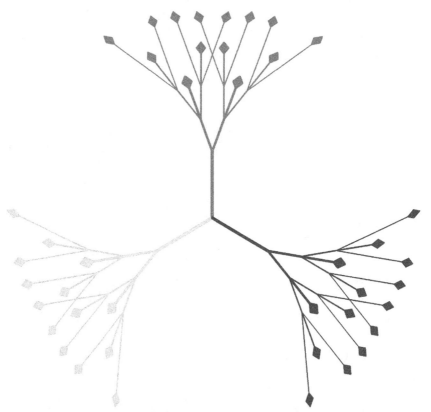

Figure 5.24: Example 4, top view

----------------------------> **Example 5** <----------------------------

Angle 22.5
DEPTH 6
SHRINK 0.7
STEP 0.3
COLOR 80 70 0
COLOR 0 255 0
COLOR 40 30 0
MACRO "Branch" [&F "Leaf" V "Bush"]
Axiom C0 "Bush"
ERP "Internode" ///// F
Production "Bush" (Branch) ////// (Branch) ////// (Branch)
Production "Internode" F "Twig"
Production "Leaf" [C1 &&& {+S-SS-S+|+S-SS-S}]
Production <0.5> "Twig" [C2 + & VV F]
Production <0.5> "Twig" [C2 - ^ V V F]

This example is inspired by a lovely bush that appears in *The Algorithmic Beauty of Plants*. It is much prettier than the four purely tutorial examples seen so far. I'll just point out some features to note. No expansions are shown here because they grow unwieldy by just the second iteration. Figures 5.25 and 5.26 on the next page are side and top views of the bush.

- The same technique as shown in the prior example is used to create three diverging Branches: the Bush production rolls around the central axis, and the Branch macro pitches forward.

- Three realistic colors are used: brown (C0) for the main branches, bright green (C1) for leaves, and dark brown (C2) for small side twigs.

- The use of the Internode production for the ERP, rather than simply placing the Internode definition in the ERP, delays expansion of the Internode commands, producing a more compact and visually pleasing bush. Offsetting commands by using an extra production like this is a useful technique.

- I randomly distribute twigs on two sides of the main stems and doubly shrink them (VV) relative to their source stem.

Figure 5.25: Example 5, side view

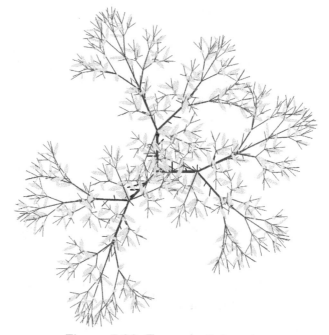

Figure 5.26: Example 5, top view

--------------------------------> **Example 6** <----------------------------

```
Angle 22.5
DEPTH 5
SHRINK 0.9
STEP 0.5
AZIMUTH 180
ELEVATION 10
COLOR 80 70 0
COLOR 0 255 0
COLOR 255 0 0
Axiom C0 "Plant"
Production "Plant" "Internode" + [V"Plant" + "Flower"] -- [V"Plant"] //
      [--"Leaf"] "Internode" - [V"Plant" "Flower"] ++ V"Plant"
Production "Internode" VF "Seg" [//&& "Leaf"] [//^^ "Leaf"] VF "Seg"
Production "Seg" "Seg" F "Seg"
Production "Leaf" [C1 {+SS-SSS-SS+|+SS-SSS-SS}]
Production "Flower" [ F &&&& "Petal" ---- "Petal" ---- "Petal" ---- "Petal" ]
Production "Petal" [C2 {+SS-S-SS+|+SS-S-SS}]
```

This example, like the prior bush, is inspired by a gorgeous flower that appears in *The Algorithmic Beauty of Plants*. I modified the shape of the plant to more evenly space branching (perhaps in defiance of nature!), and I modified the flower to be more distinctive (though without the subtle beauty of the original). No expansions are shown here because they grow unwieldy by just the second iteration. Figure 5.27 on Page 143 portrays this flower, which also decorates the front cover of this book. Note the following:

- The most basic structure of the flower is controlled by the Plant production. It starts with an Internode, which is basically a stem with a pair of leaves. Then it hangs on a step followed by a recursive plant with a flower, restores the state, hangs on another step followed by a recursive Plant, restores the state, adds a Leaf, advances with another Internode, hangs on a step with a recursive Plant and a Flower, restores the state, and ends by taking a step and appending yet another recursive Plant. You can easily modify this to your liking by using different orientation changes, adding or removing features, and so forth.

- The Internode production takes a step, then takes one or more steps with Seg, attaches a pair of leaves on opposite sides of the stem, takes another step, and finally more stepping with Seg.

- The Seg production is worthy of study, because it is useful for many plants. It is responsible for having lower branches (those that appear in earlier iterations) longer than peripheral branches, as is natural for a plant. The first time it expands it becomes Seg F Seg, and only F moves the turtle. With the next expansion we have three F moves, and so forth, exponentially lengthening the Internode as iterations progress.

- The Leaf and the Petal are straightforward filled planes, the leaf colored green and the petal colored red.

- The Flower takes a step forward to put it out on a little stem apart from the supporting stem, making the flower more prominent. The Petals are most visible if they are perpendicular to this little stem, so &&&& pitches the turtle forward 4 * 22.5 = 90 degrees. After the first petal is drawn we turn right 90 degrees, draw another petal, turn again, draw the third, turn again and draw the last.

Figure 5.27: The flower from example 6

Index

www.ingramcontent.com/pod-product-compliance
Lightning Source LLC
La Vergne TN
LVHW081345050326
832903LV00024B/1328